flaminio gundy

Toulouse

Capital of Occitania

Toulouse
Capital of Occitania

by Flaminio Gundy

Kindle Direct Publishing, USA, 2023

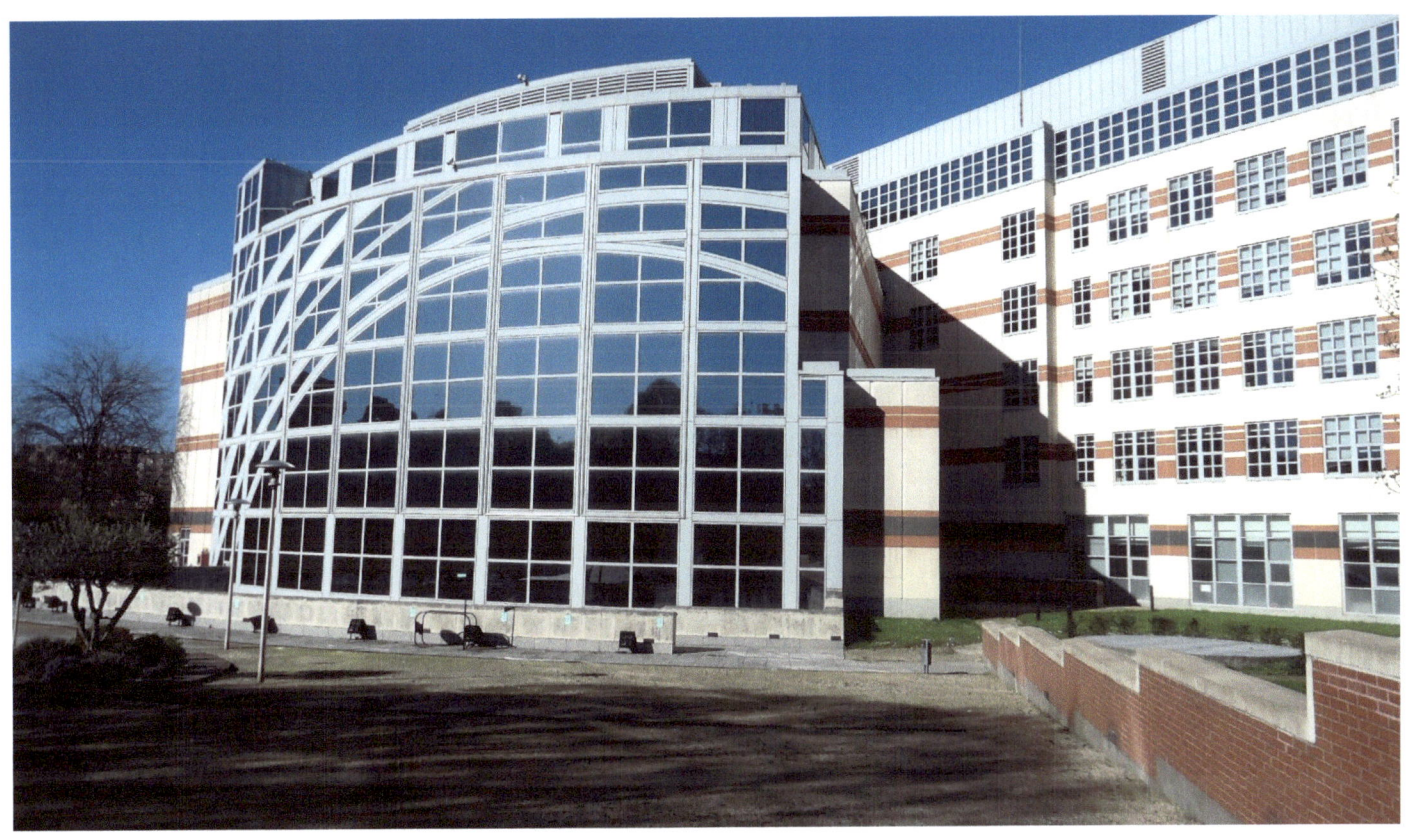

In the heart of Haute Garonne lies the city of Toulouse. It represents the center of the south-west of France, one of the most loved in the whole nation, perhaps due to its surprisingly Mediterranean climate, also influenced by the serene temperament of the citizens of nearby Spain who have lived in this city for many centuries.

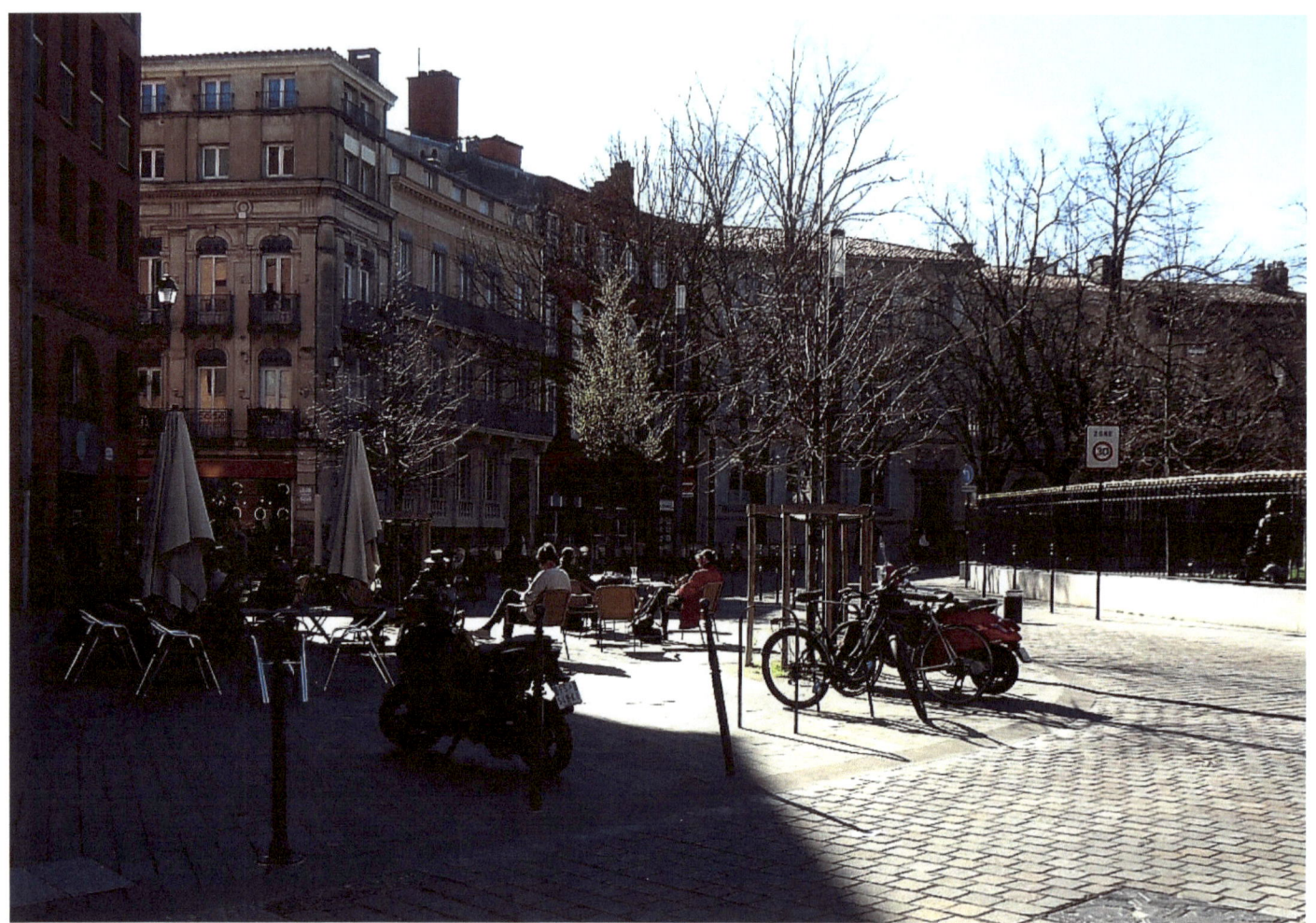

Place Saint-Sernin

Toulouse was called this by the Romans when they conquered it between 120 and 100 BC. and later under the reign of Emperor Augustus the city was moved a few kilometers from the hills to the banks of the Garonne, the river that crosses it, making it a classic French city to be visited both on foot, along the banks of the river, and on board a boat.

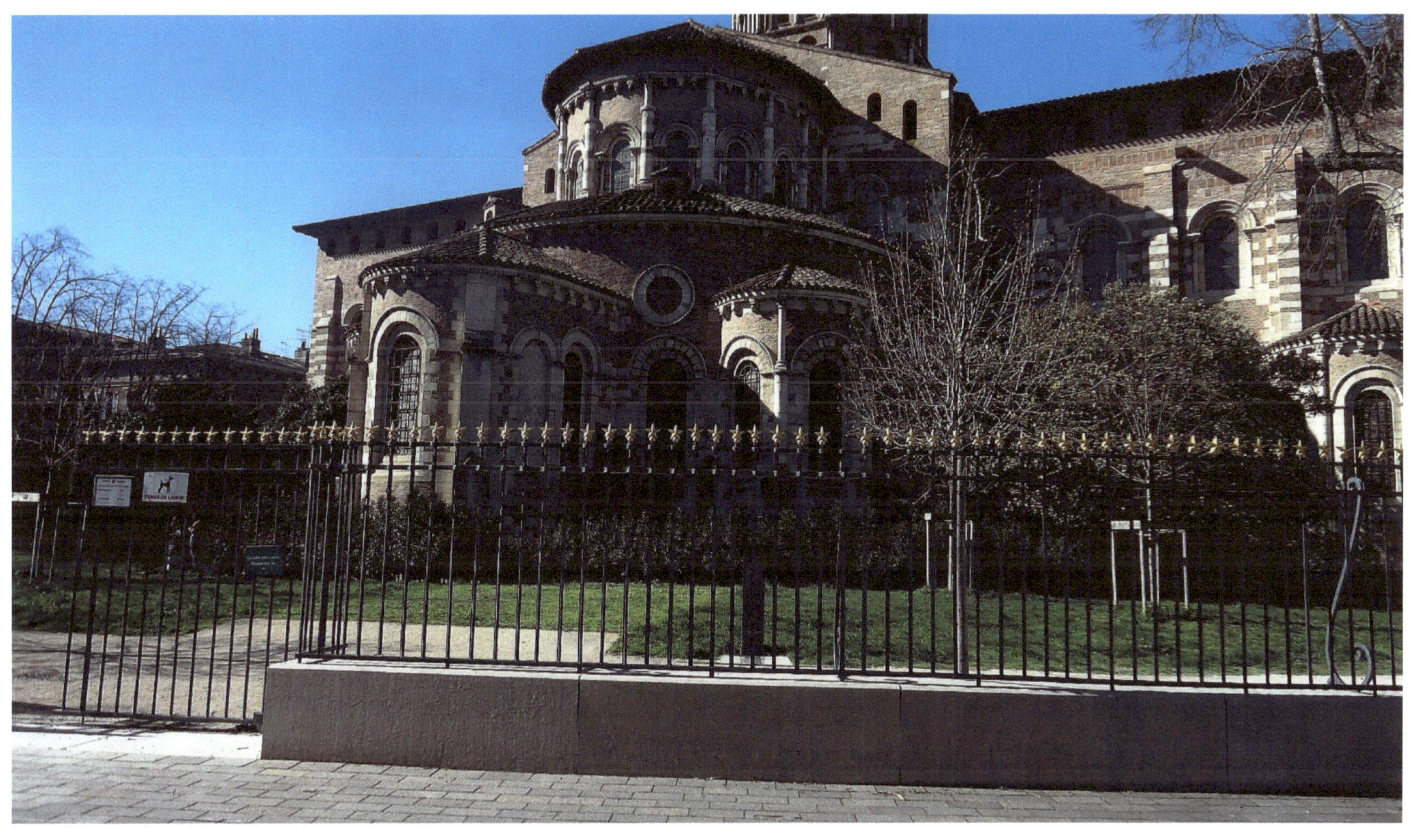

Basilique de Saint-Sernin de Toulouse

The first bishop of Toulouse was Saturninus, venerated as a holy martyr by the Catholic Church because after his refusal to sacrifice to Jupiter Capitolinus he was tied by the pagan residents to the neck of a bull, which fled furiously and tore him to death in 257 AD. C. The basilica of Saint-Sernin in Toulouse was built on the site where his remains were found.

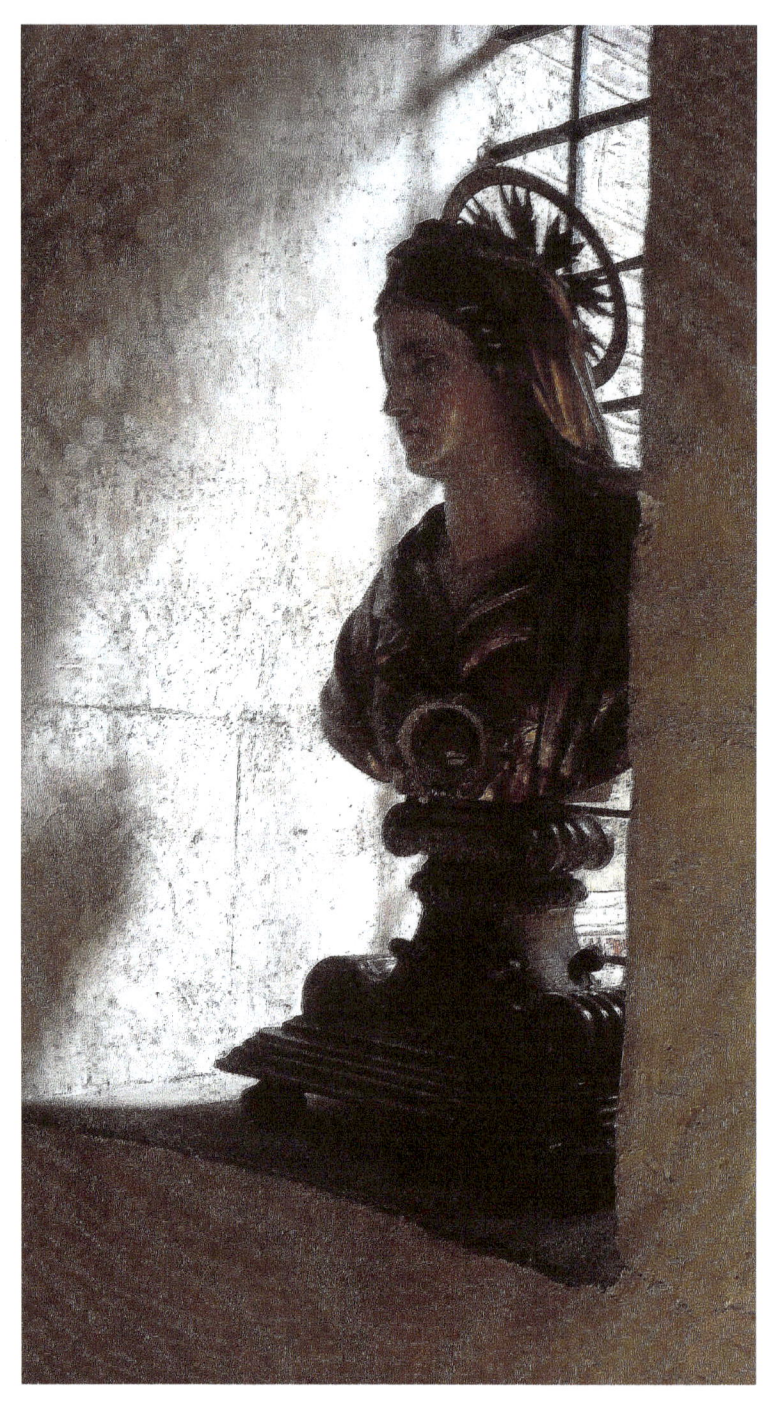

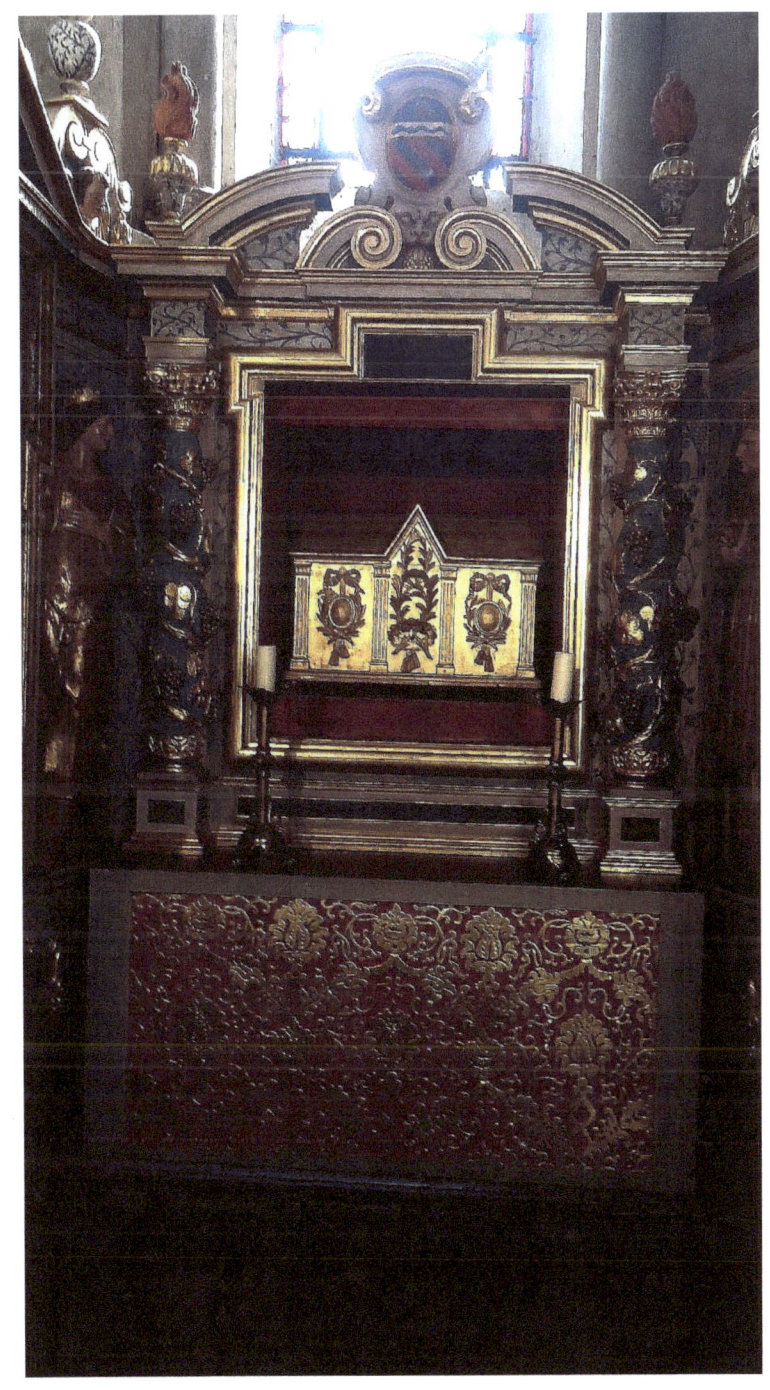

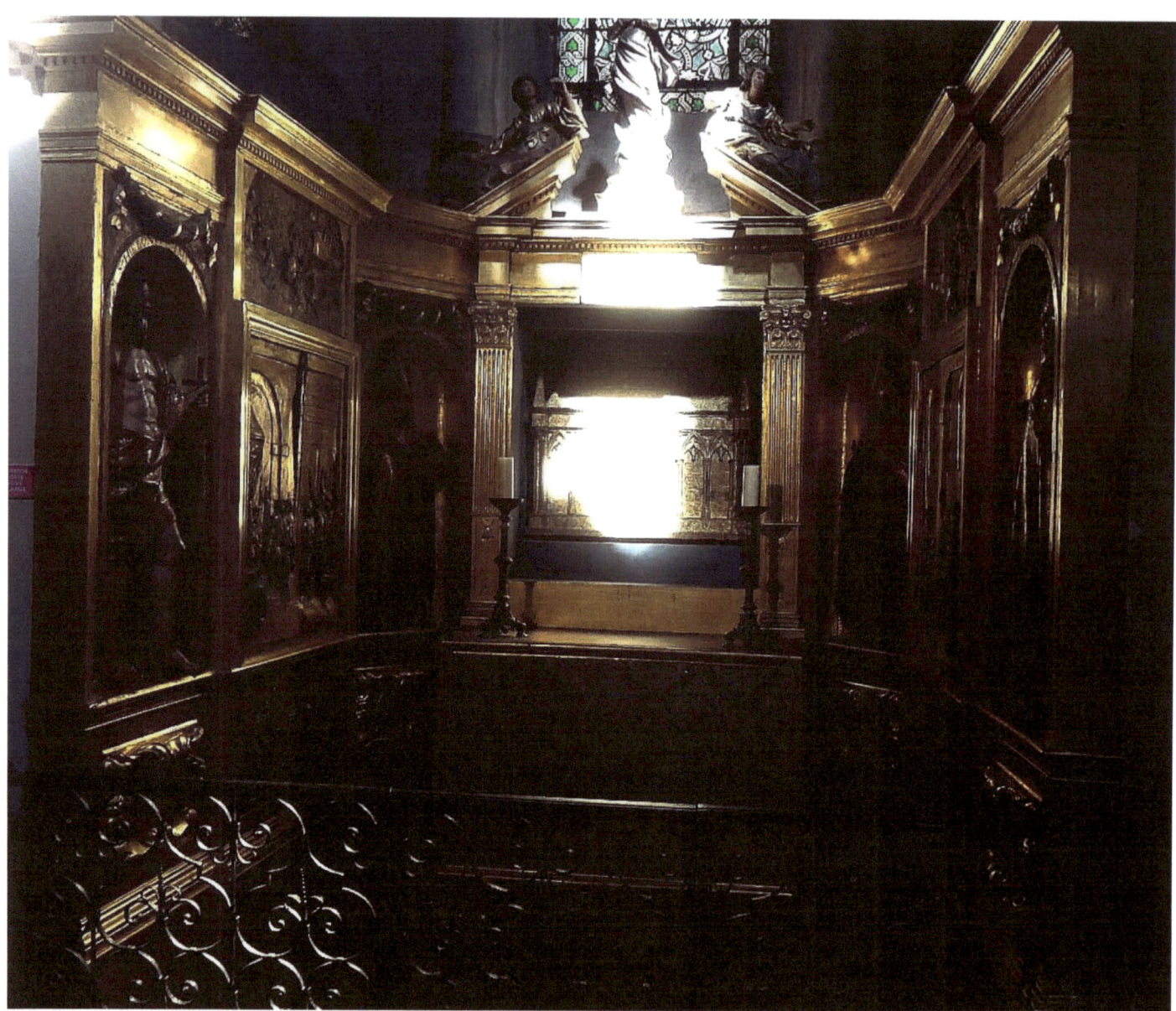

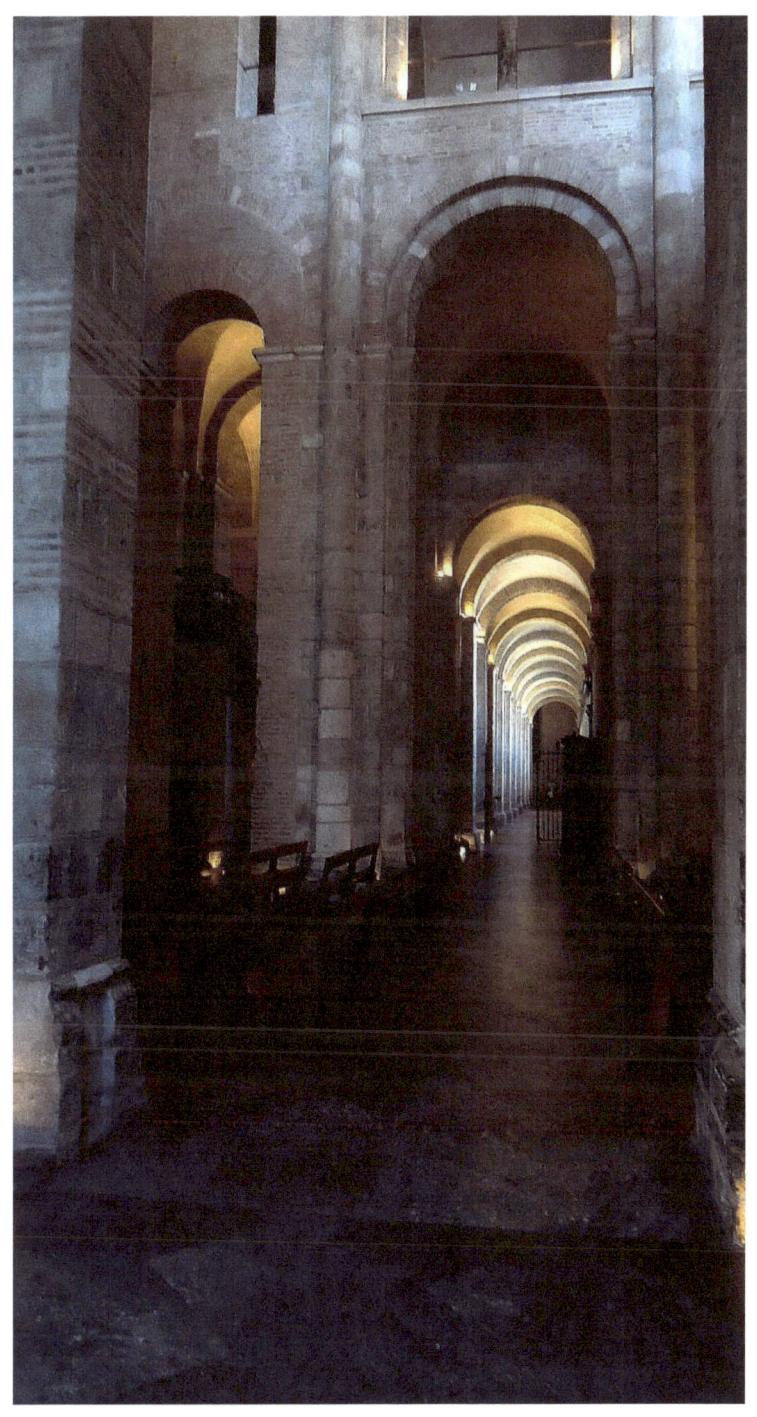

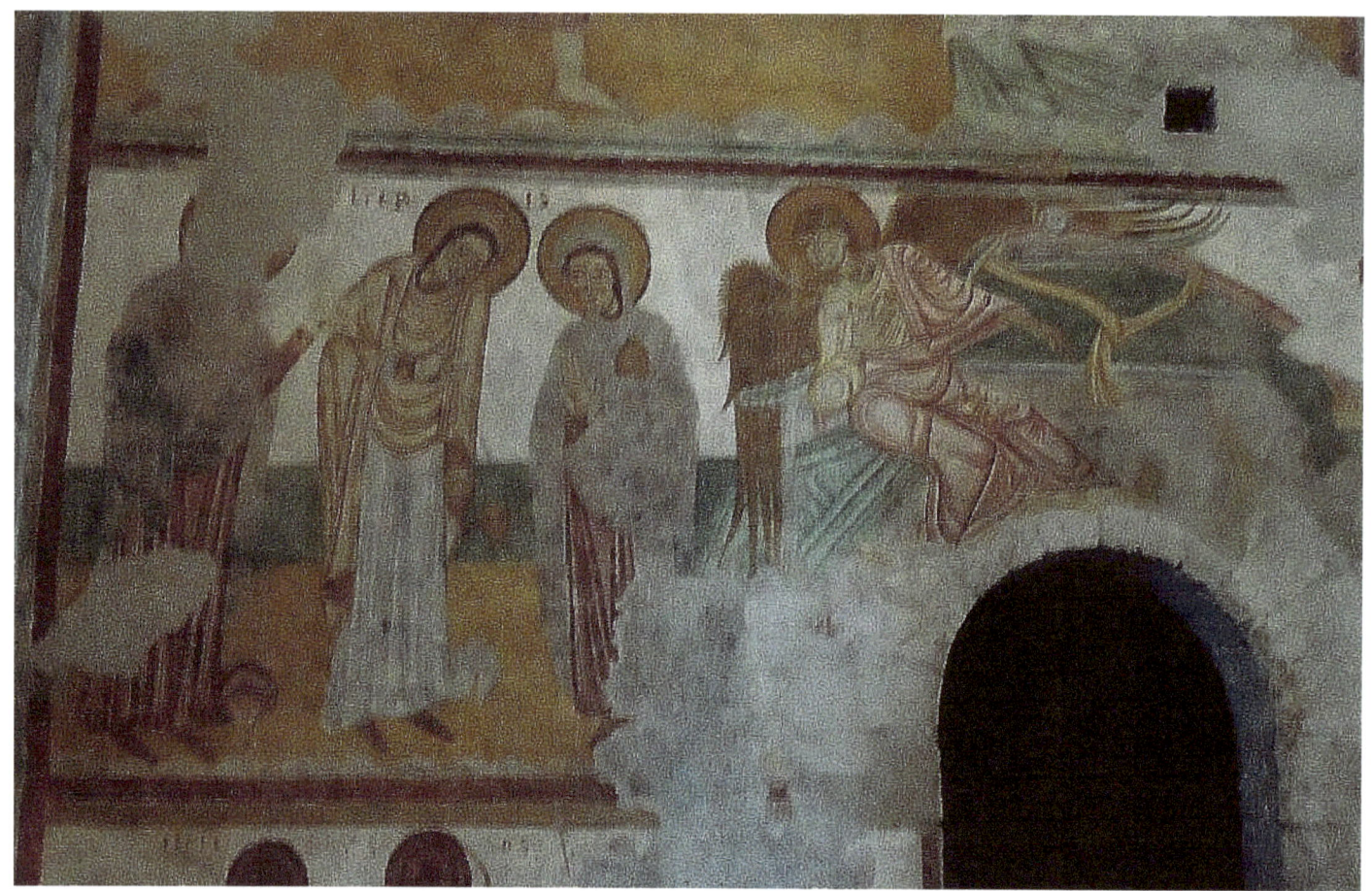

Also called the cultural capital of Occitania, Toulouse is a city where good living is reflected in the local gastronomy, with characteristic products of France such as Foie Gras, the goose liver inevitable on the tables of the French, or cheeses, such as the tasty Roquefort, with a strong smell and strong flavor and the Rocamadour goat's cheese.

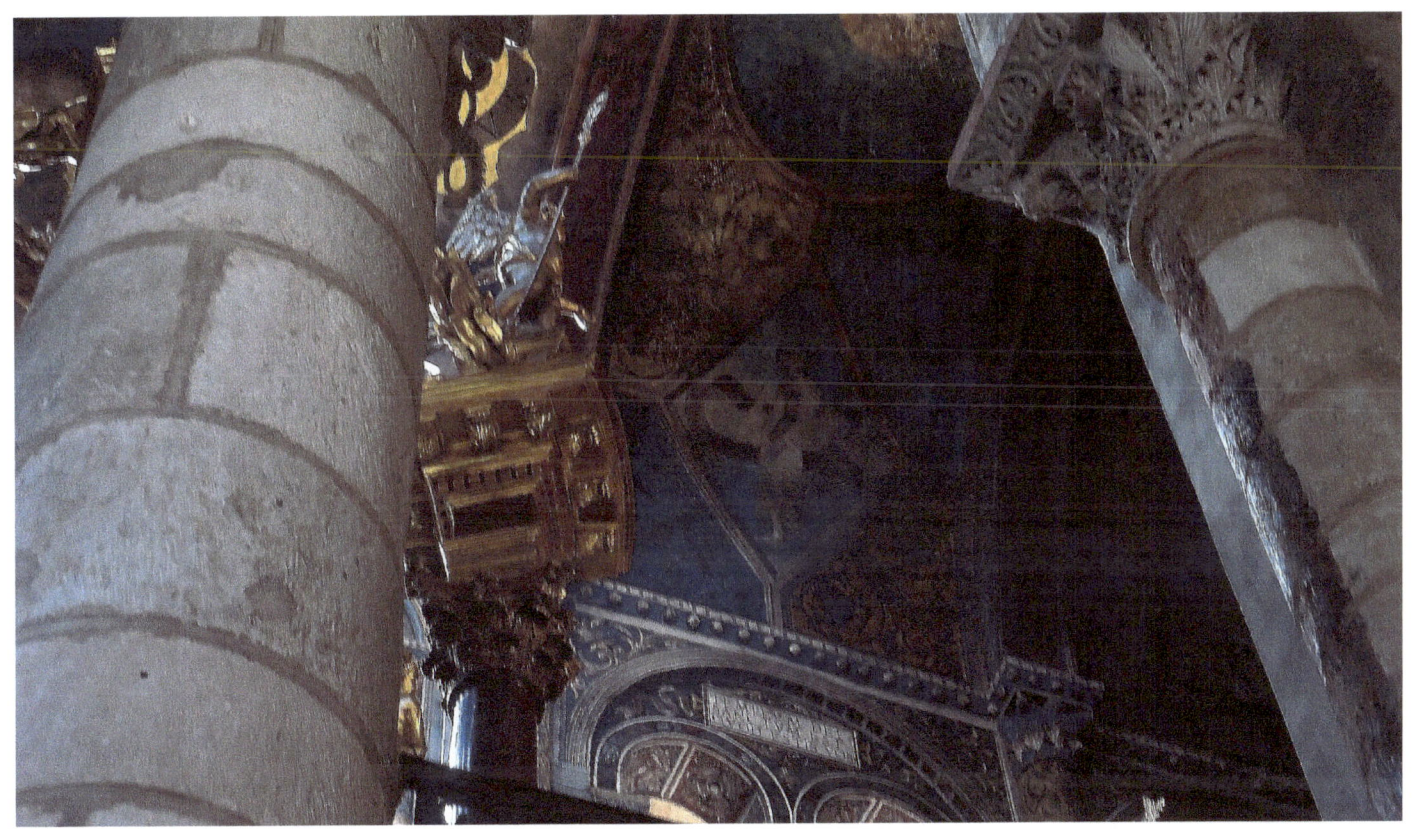

Another specialty of Toulouse cuisine is duck, prepared both in the form of Foie Gras and as a fillet, the famous "Magret", or even "confit", i.e. the meat that is preserved in the fat from its own cooking.

The second typical dish of the city of Toulouse is certainly the "Cassoulet": based on pork, duck and sausage and flavored with white beans, it is cooked for a long time in a terracotta casserole, from which it takes its name and au gratin with a thick layer of breadcrumbs.

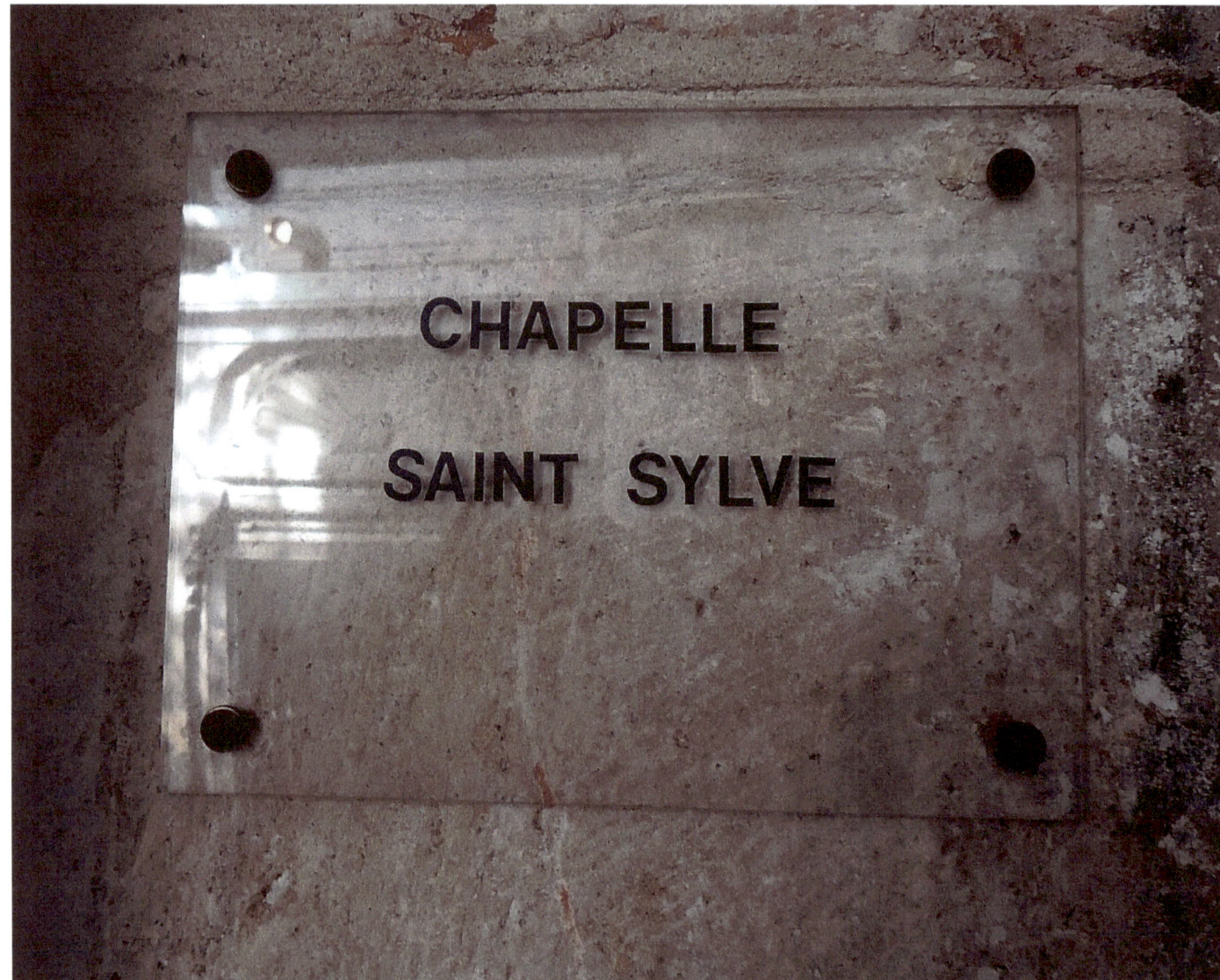

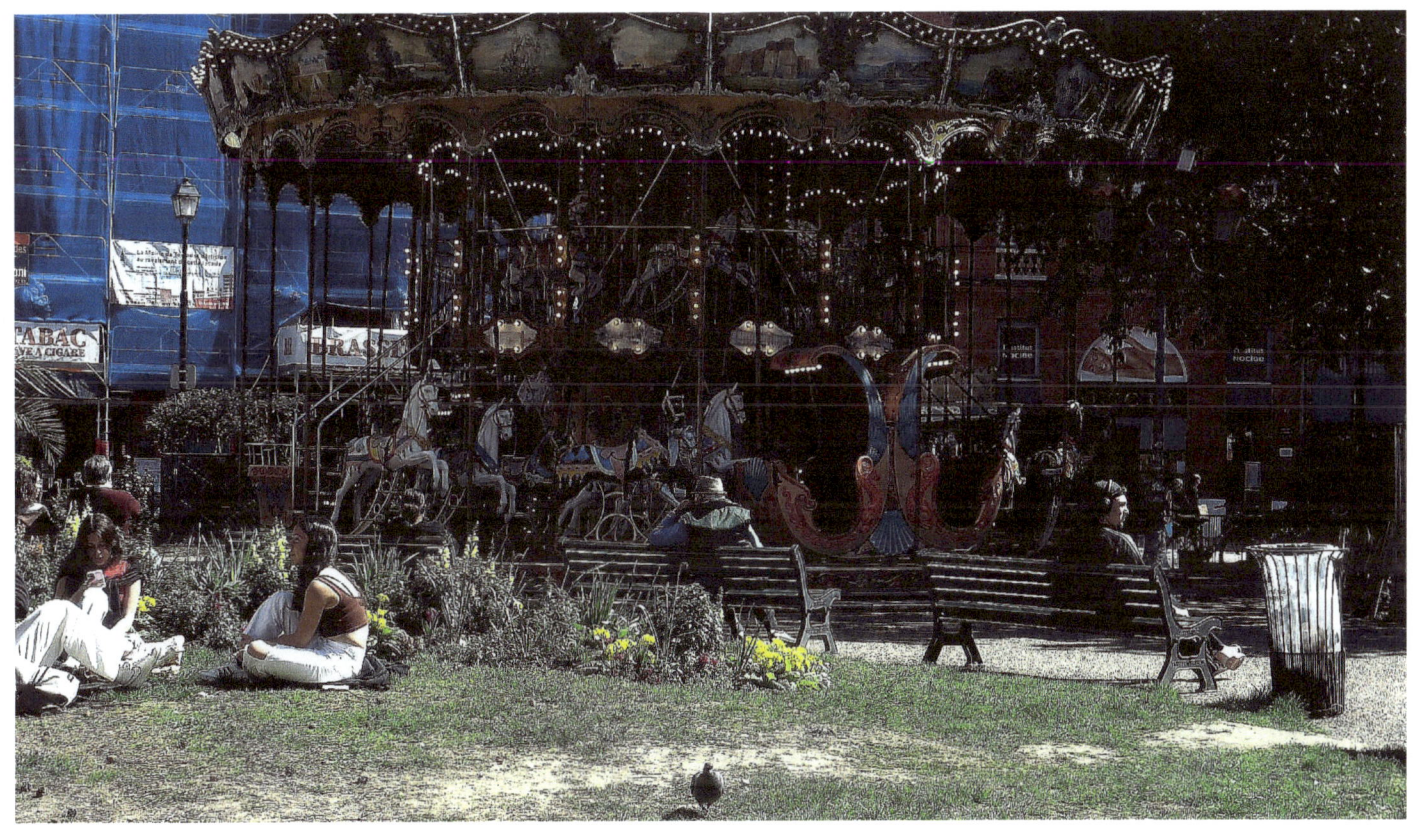

In February, in the most beautiful square in the city, Place du Capitol, there is also a festival dedicated to the violet, which is in bloom precisely in this period, where not only sweets, but many other preparations, such as jams, liqueurs and perfumes as masters of the whole party.

The whole square is adorned with purple balloons and themed decorations always in this splendid colour.

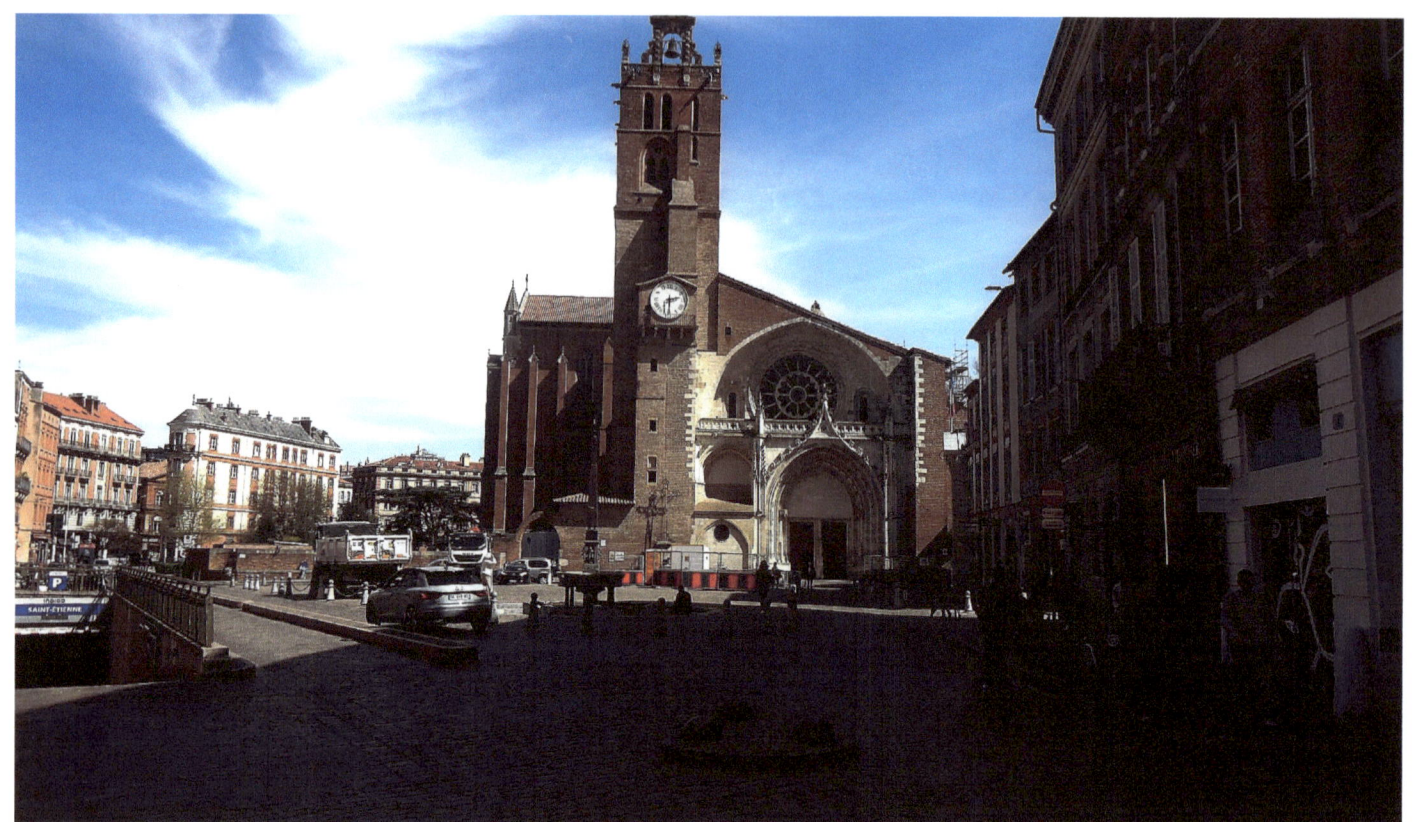

Cathédrale Saint-Étienne

There are three covered markets in Toulouse, but the largest is the Marché Victor Hugo, located in a building inaugurated way back in 1892, with around a hundred stalls, located on the ground floor, while on the first floor there are five restaurants open only for lunch and above there is a paid parking.
The market is open every day, except Monday, from 7am to 2pm.

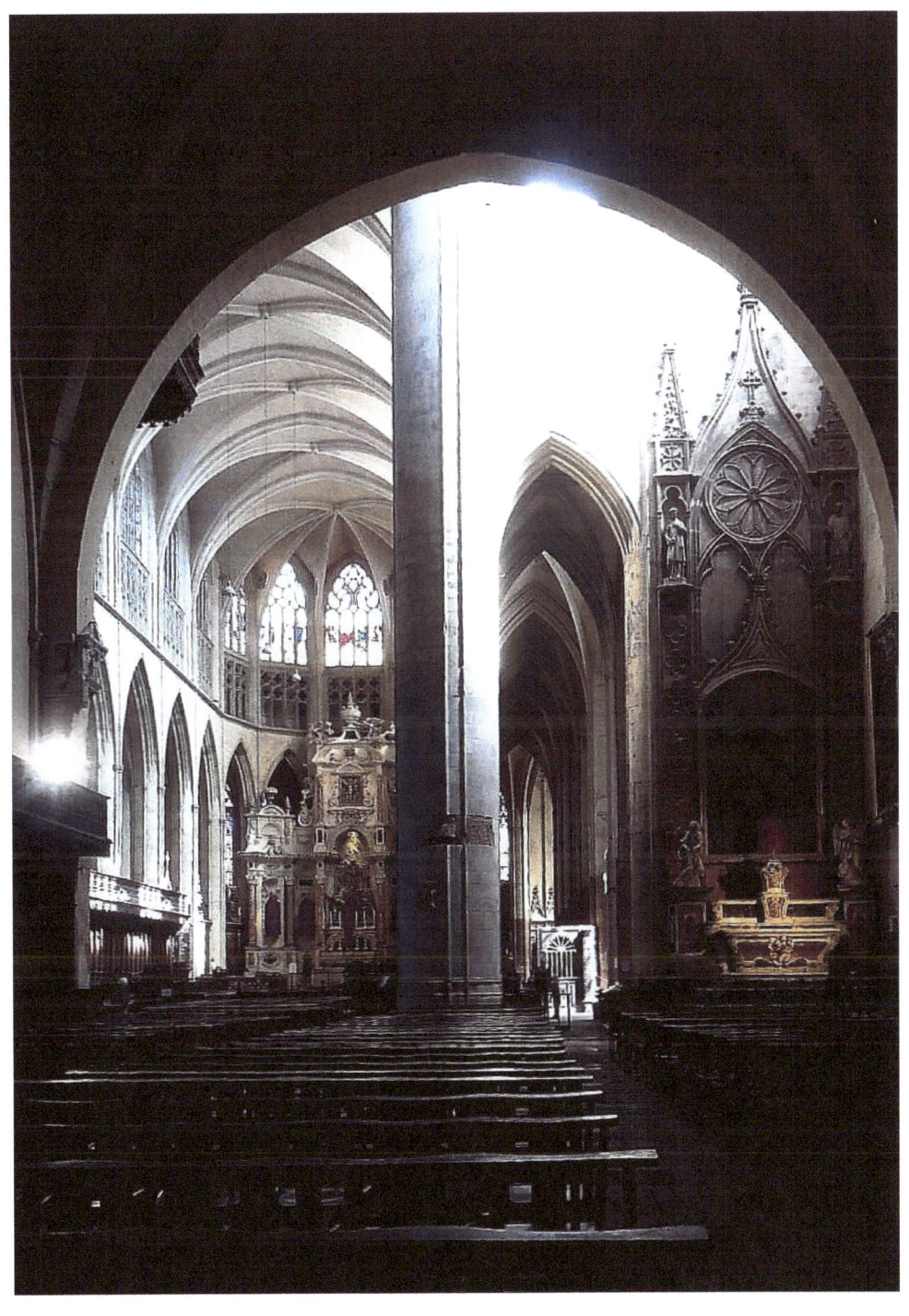

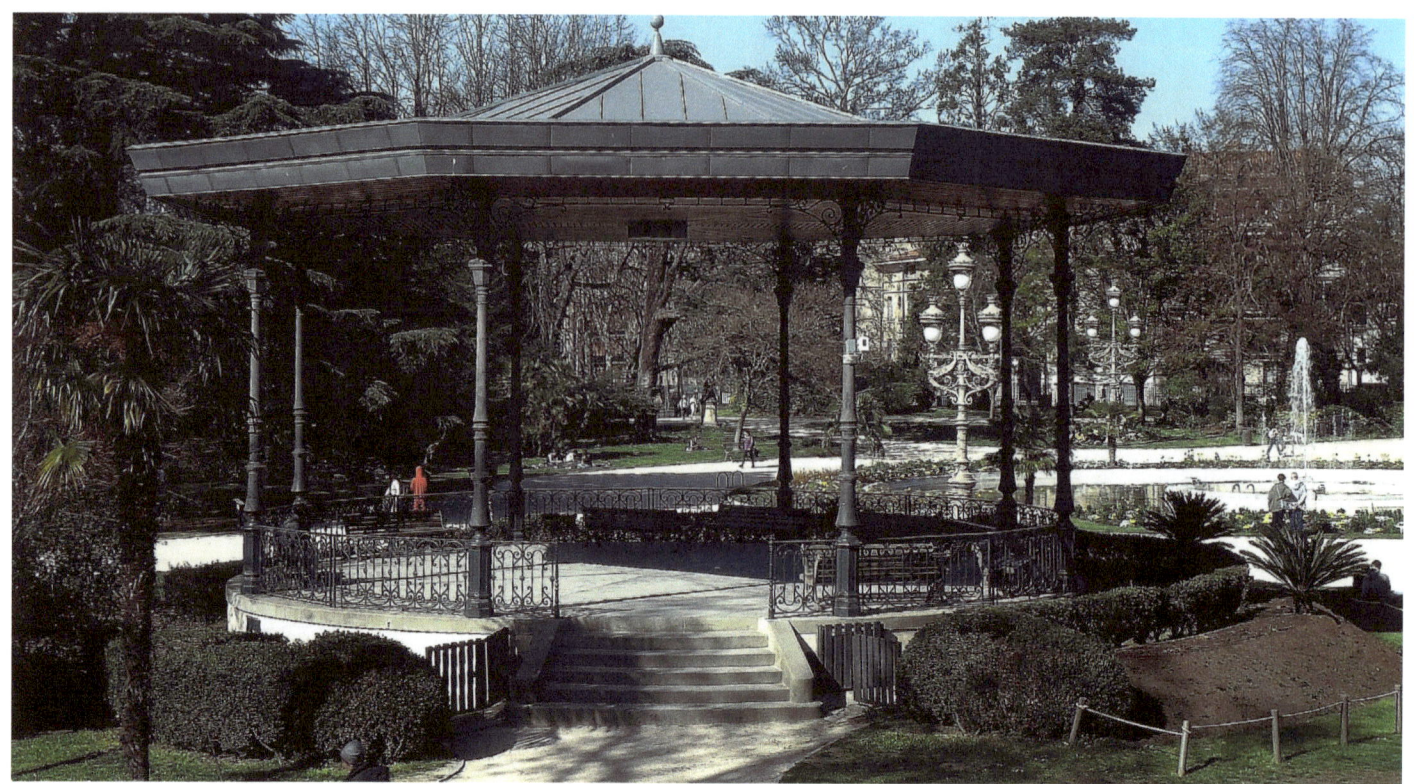

Toulouse was the capital of the Visigothic kingdom until 507, then of the kingdom of Aquitaine and in the 8th century of the County of Toulouse. At the time of the Muslim invasion of the Iberian Peninsula and southern France, the Arab troops suffered their first defeat at the hands of the Duke of Aquitaine, Odo the Great, in the Battle of Toulouse, in 721.

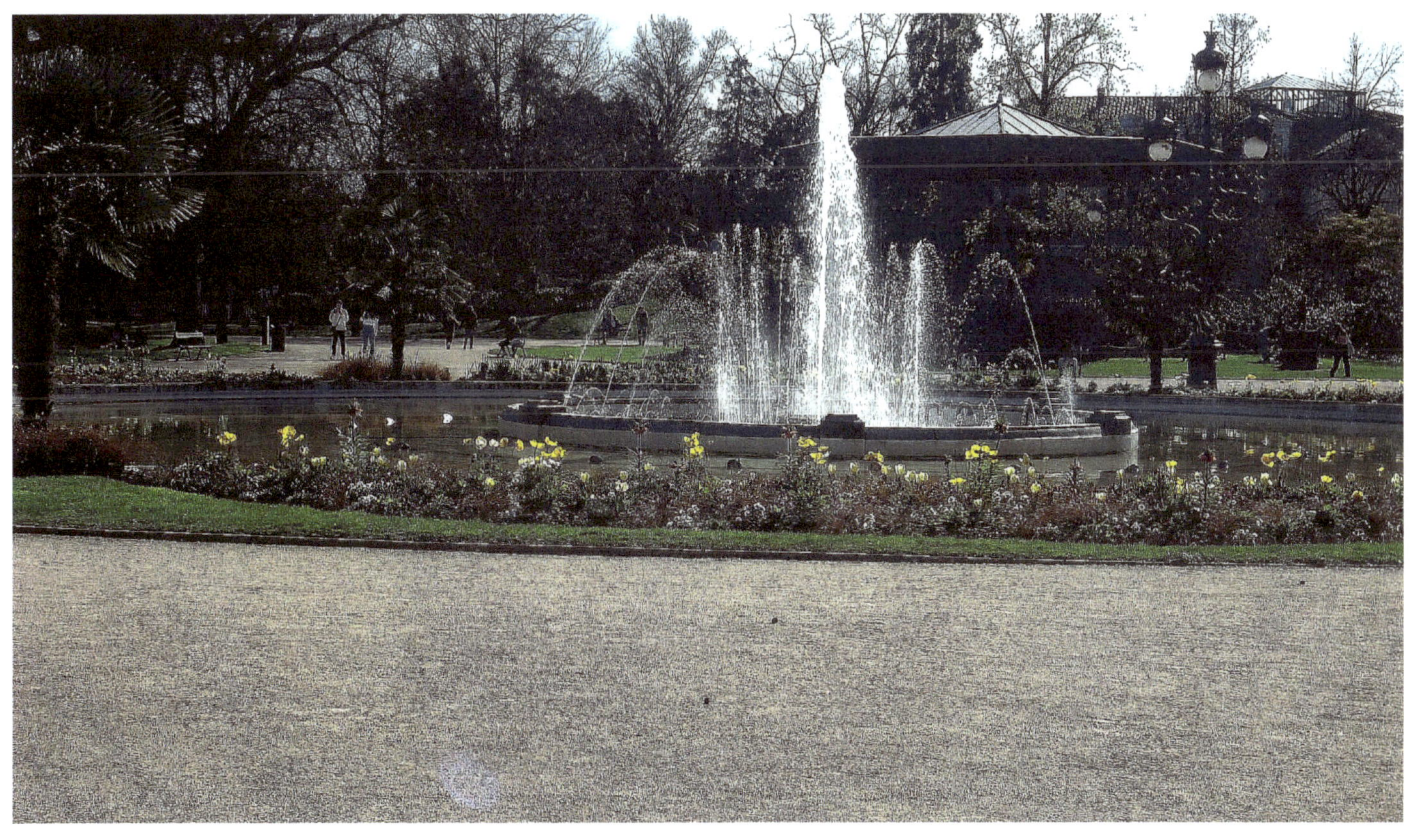

Starting from the 12th century in this region of France, a new conception of Christianity developed in disagreement with the Roman Catholic Church: Catharism, but the followers of this new religion were persecuted and condemned en masse.

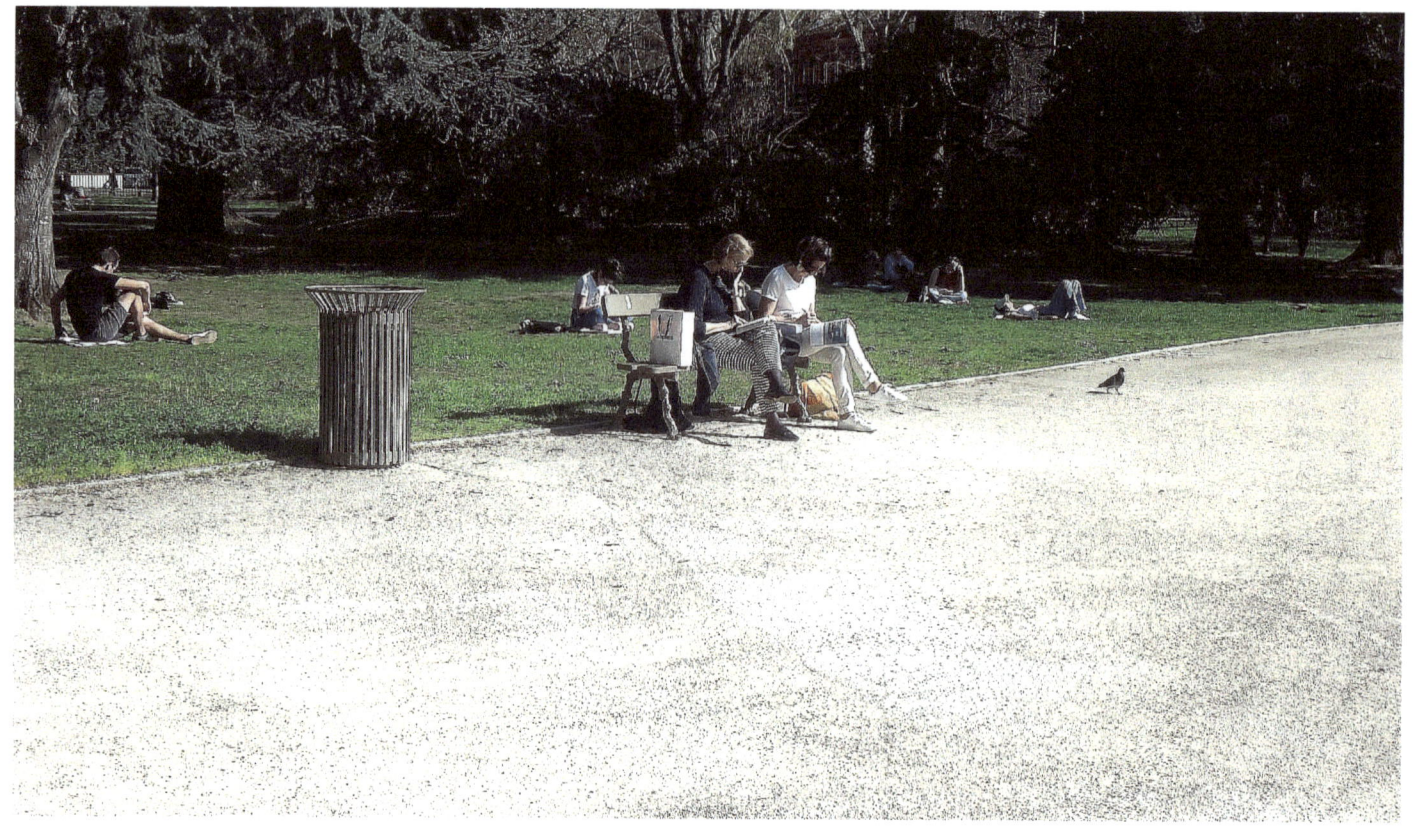

In 1215, the Spanish priest Dominic of Guzmán founded the Order of Friars Preachers (Dominicans) in Toulouse, a community of friars to combat the spread of Catharism.

In 1229 the king of France and the Pope ordered the creation of the University of Toulouse with the idea of training an elite capable of intellectually fighting Catharism.

Since 1369 the bones of the famous Dominican theologian Thomas Aquinas have rested in the church of the Jacobins of Toulouse, to honor the city as the cradle of the Dominican order in the previous century.

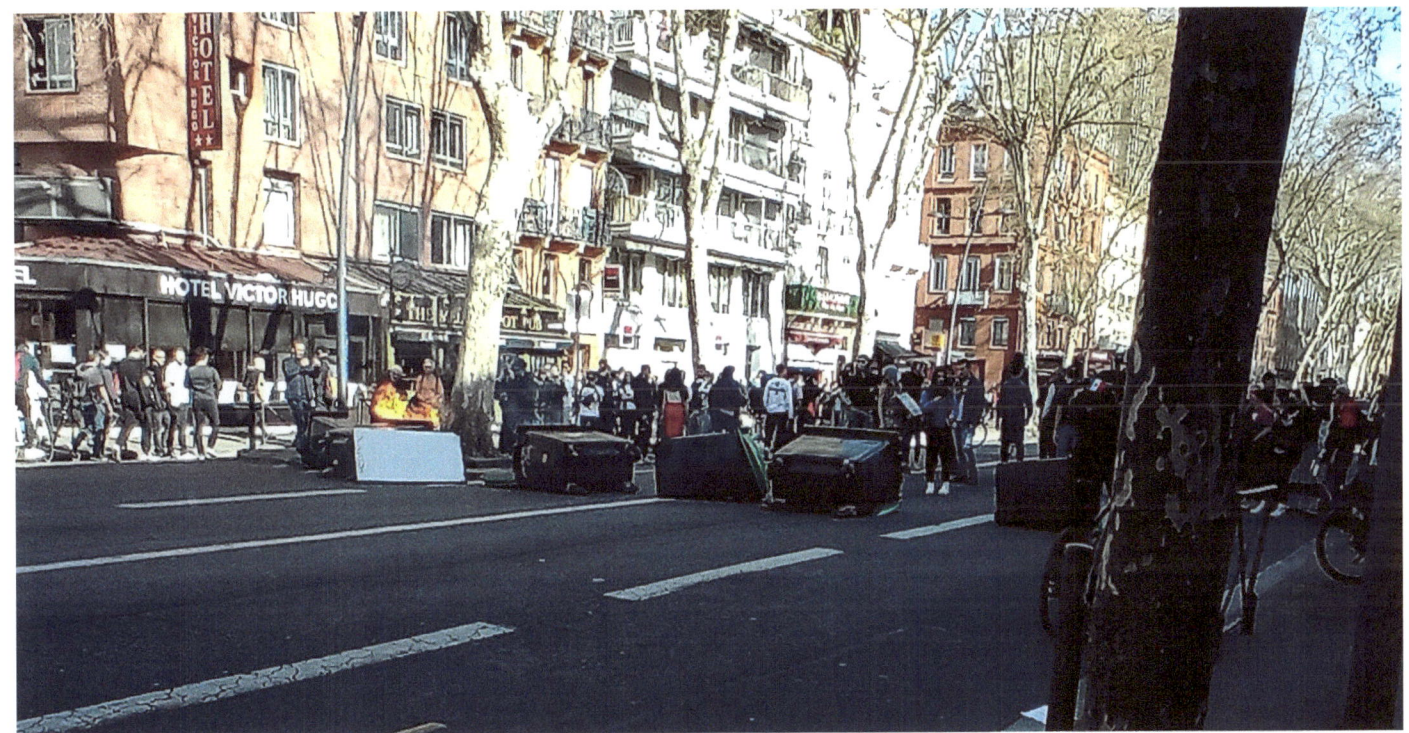

March 28, 2023

Cassoulet is undoubtedly the most popular dish on the tables of Toulouse and the nearby Languedoc region. Its name derives from the container in which it is cooked for a long time, a deep terracotta casserole with thick edges. Preparing cassoulet takes a long time, but the result will be an invigorating and substantial dish, perfect for cold winter days.

It is obtained with some essential ingredients and others that vary depending on the creativity of the chef and above all on his origin. The fact is that in Toulouse what there is no shortage of are pork, duck confit, Toulouse sausage and beans.

It is a dish of poor origins and very substantial, not really recommended in summer. During cooking in the oven, the crust that forms on the surface of the dish must be broken, even more than once.

A complicated dish, in short, but one that gives great satisfaction to foodies.

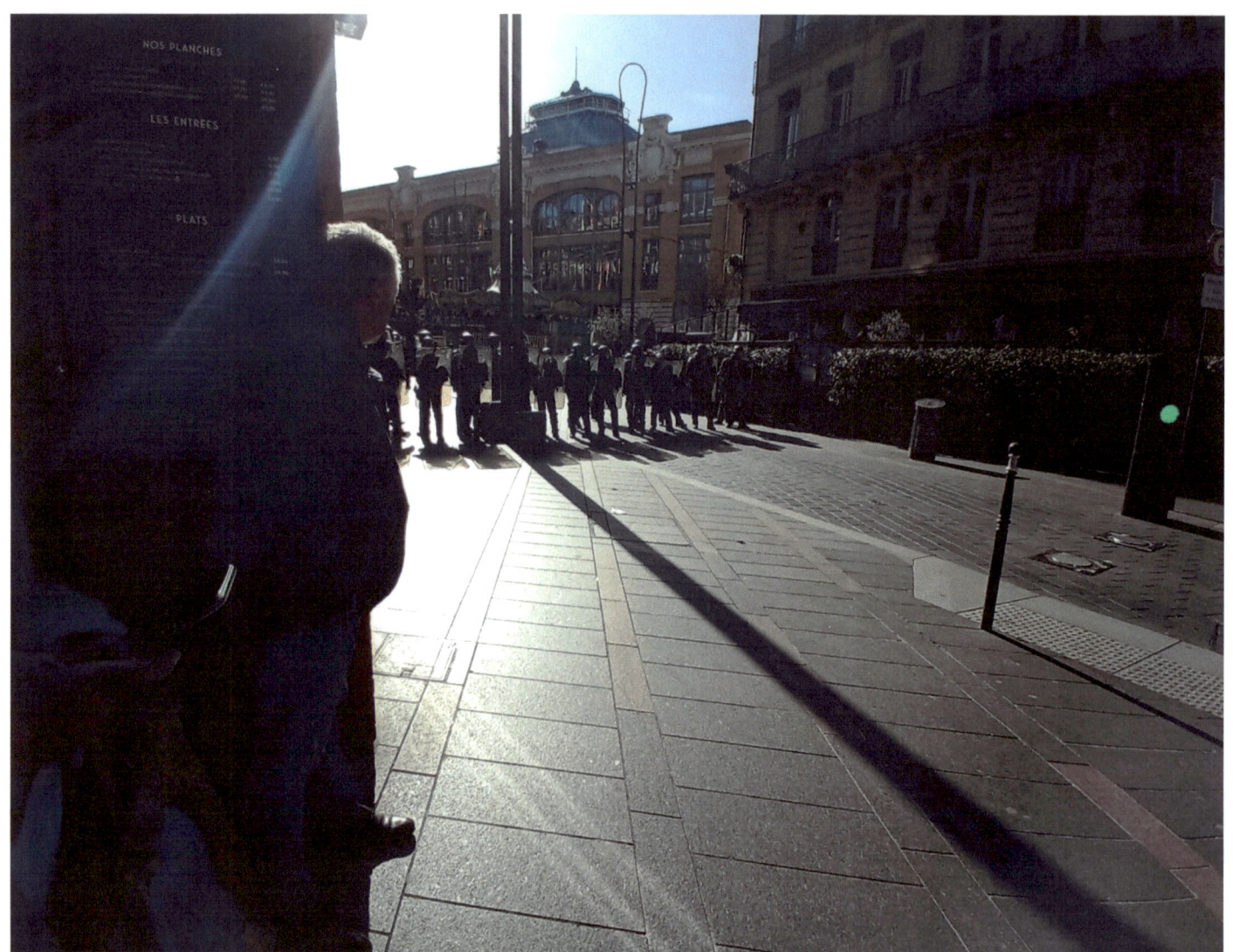

March 28, 2023

Terrine of foie gras, you must prepare it at least 5 days in advance. Goose liver can be bought in delicatessens and it is best to order it in advance. It is usually vacuum packaged and the one coming from Toulouse is excellent. The goose foie gras must be round, firm, well lobed and of a pink to yellow ocher colour. Once cooked, it will keep for a week in the refrigerator.

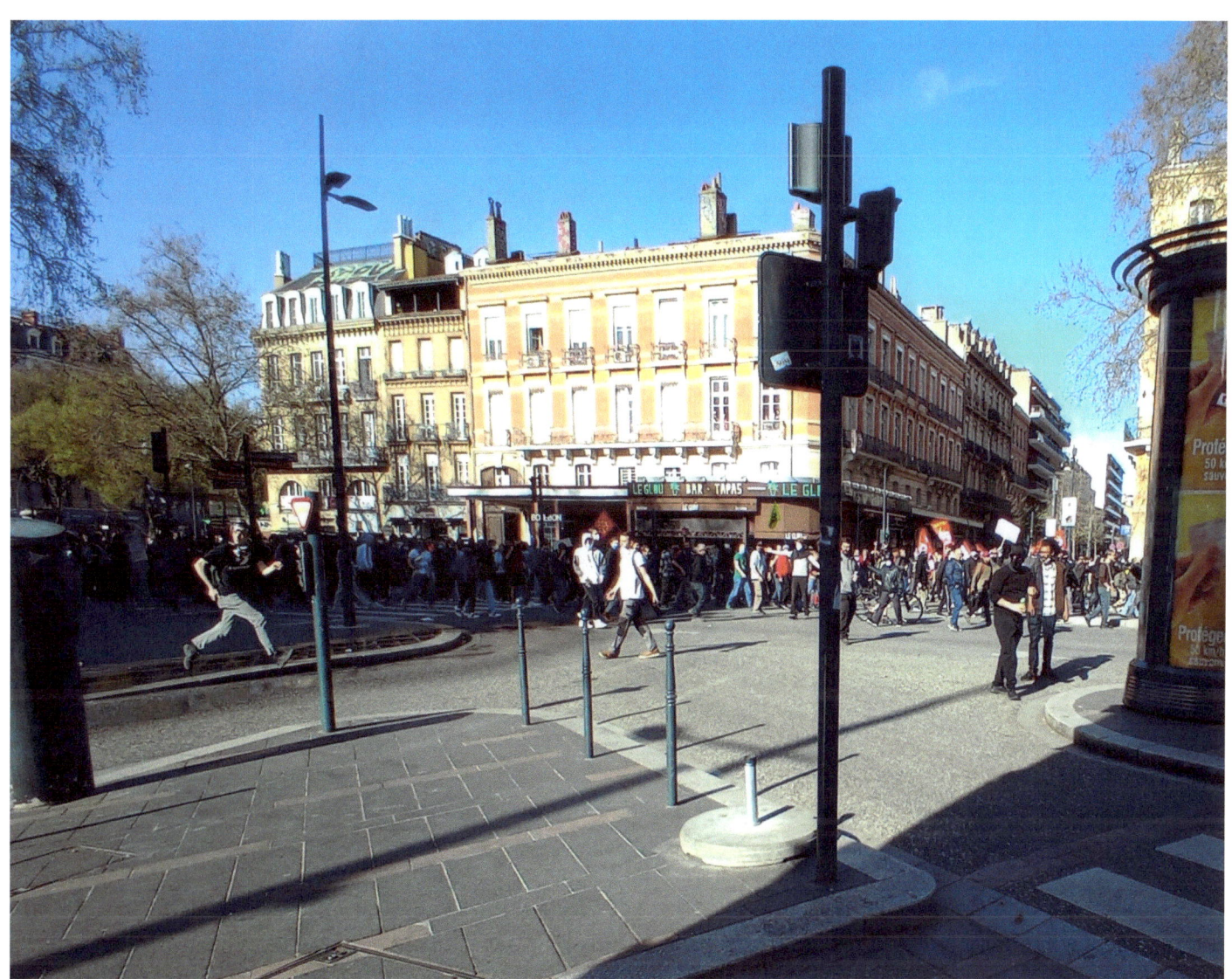

March 28, 2023

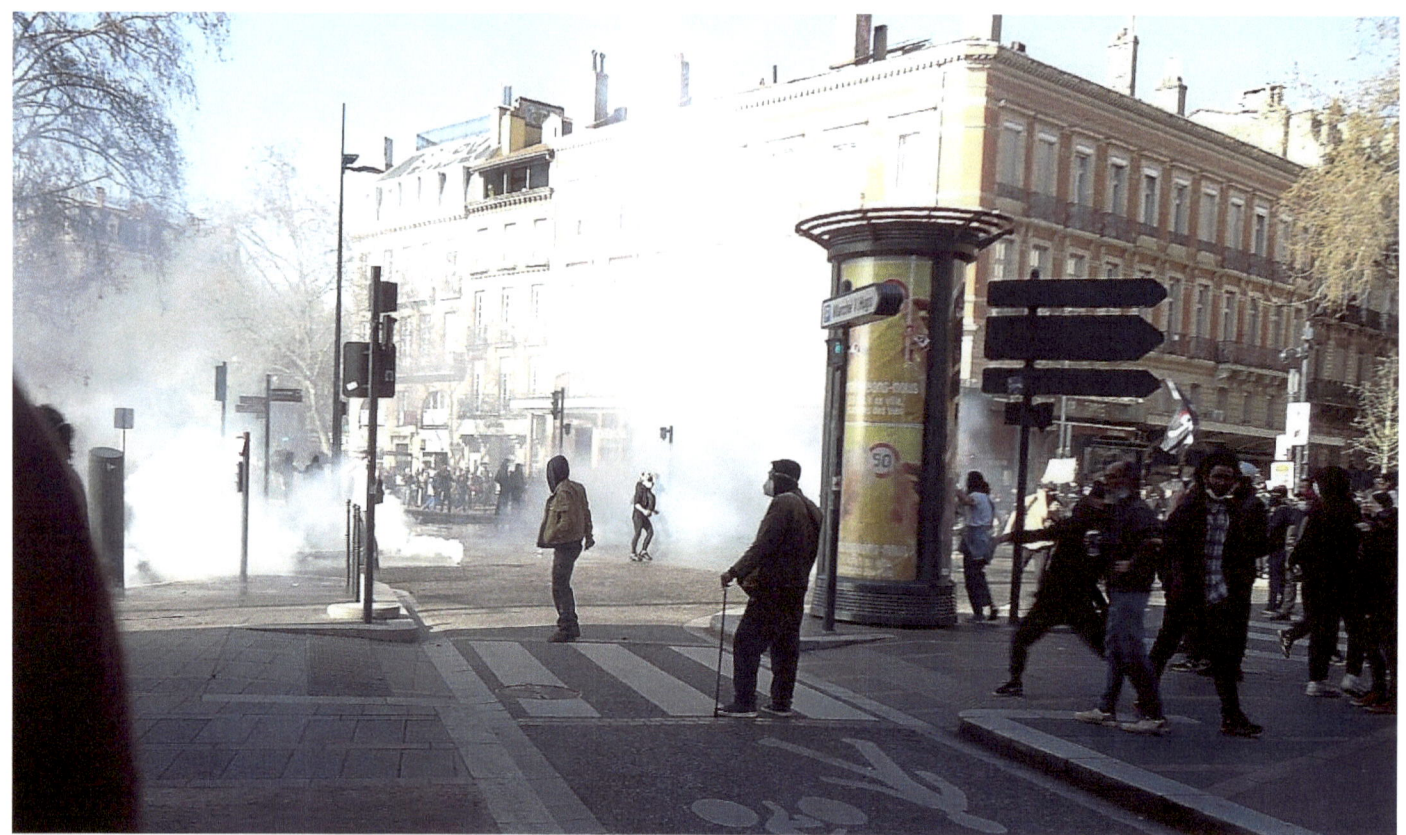

March 28, 2023

Toulouse sausage is the other great specialty of the city's gastronomy, present on market stalls since the 18th century. It is a fresh artisanal product, made with pork, salt and pepper, sold by weight and presented in a spiral. It should not contain colourants, flavors or preservatives, so it is consumed immediately and on site.

Good baked, pan-fried or grilled, this large pork sausage is offered in many restaurants in the Pink City and can be eaten in any season.

This sausage must comply with strict regulations in the various production phases. It is made up of 75% lean pork and 25% breast meat, all seasoned with salt and pepper and stuffed into natural casings. The characteristic aspect that makes it recognizable is given by the pink color and the diameter of 3 cm. Don't look for it outside of Toulouse, because it can't be found!

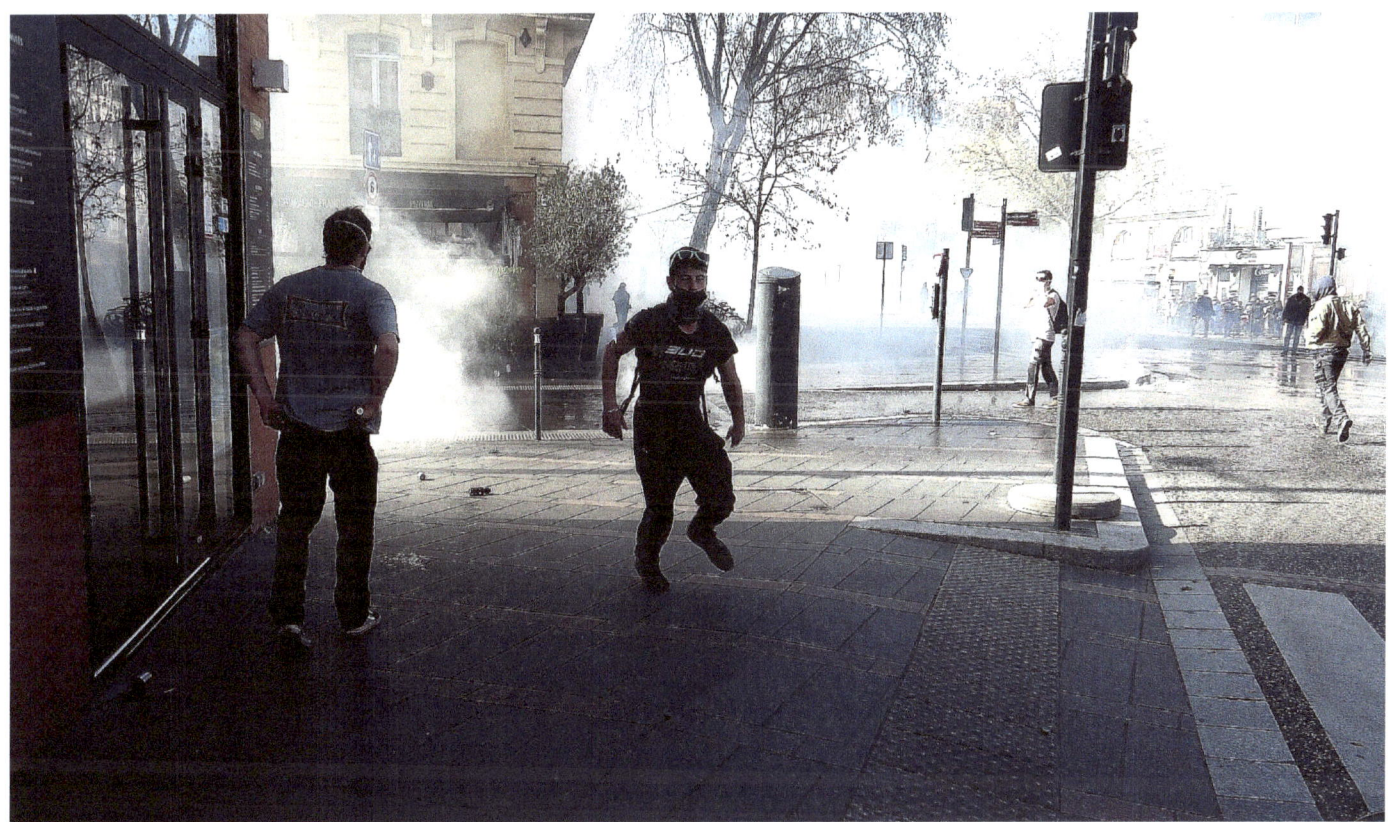

March 28, 2023

Magret sec, given that the people of Toulouse eat everything about duck, the magret - i.e. the breast - is a very prized part, although considered almost too lean by connoisseurs of the bird. Therefore, either you eat the magret in one of the infinite hot preparations, or you buy it in the sec version, that is, seasoned and vacuum-packed. Perfect gift, highly transportable. Where to buy it to make sure it is typical? Covered markets like Victor Hugo or St. Cyprien are better.

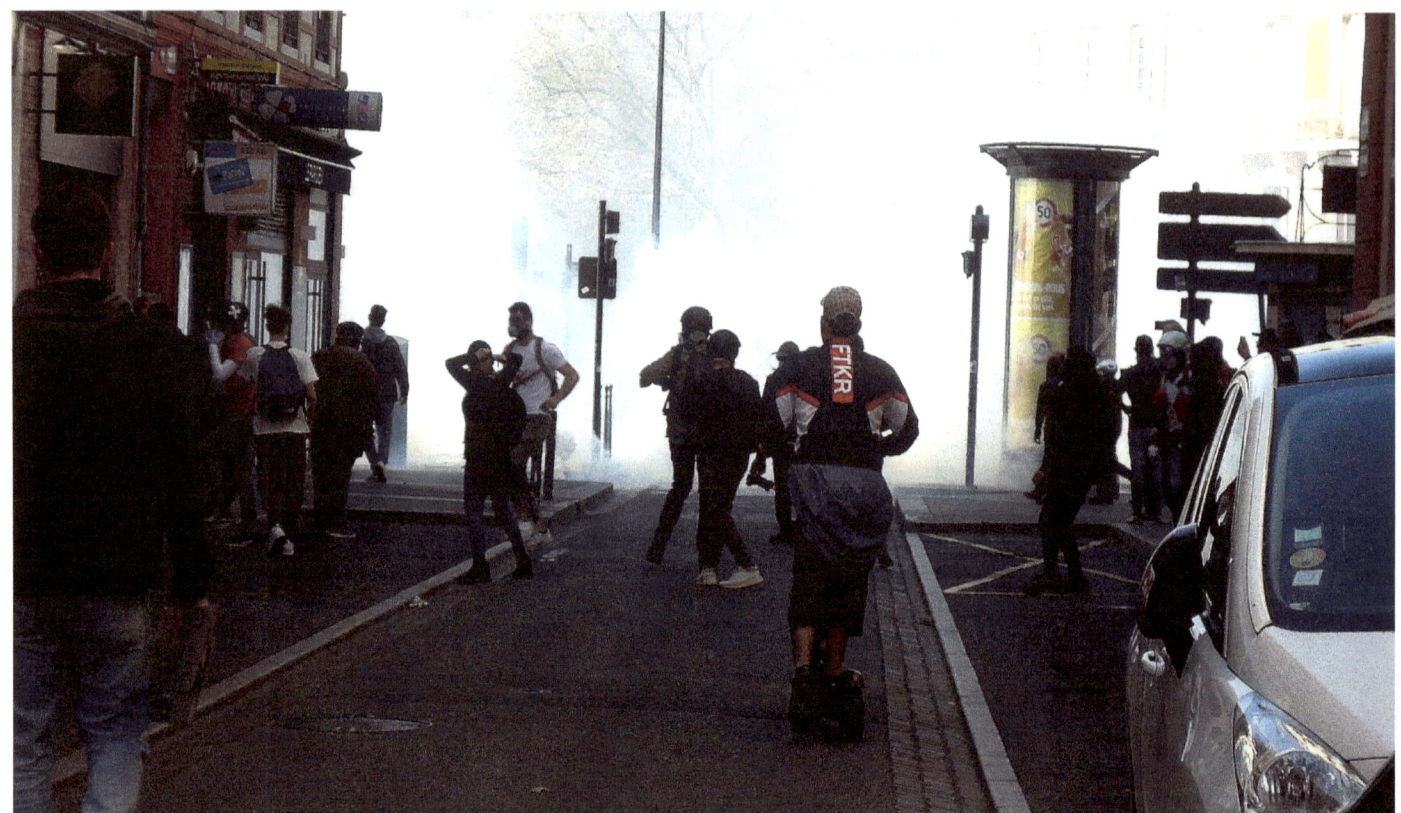

March 28, 2023

Duck alicuit is a stew made with duck neck and wings. Duck is one of the Toulouse specialities, which is offered both as foie gras - it seems that duck is better than goose - which is enjoyed with crunchy baguette, magret, or breast, and confit, where the meat is cooked and preserved in its own fat.

Duck is also one of the basic ingredients together with pork and sausage flavored with white beans, with which Cassoulet is prepared, another typical dish of the city.

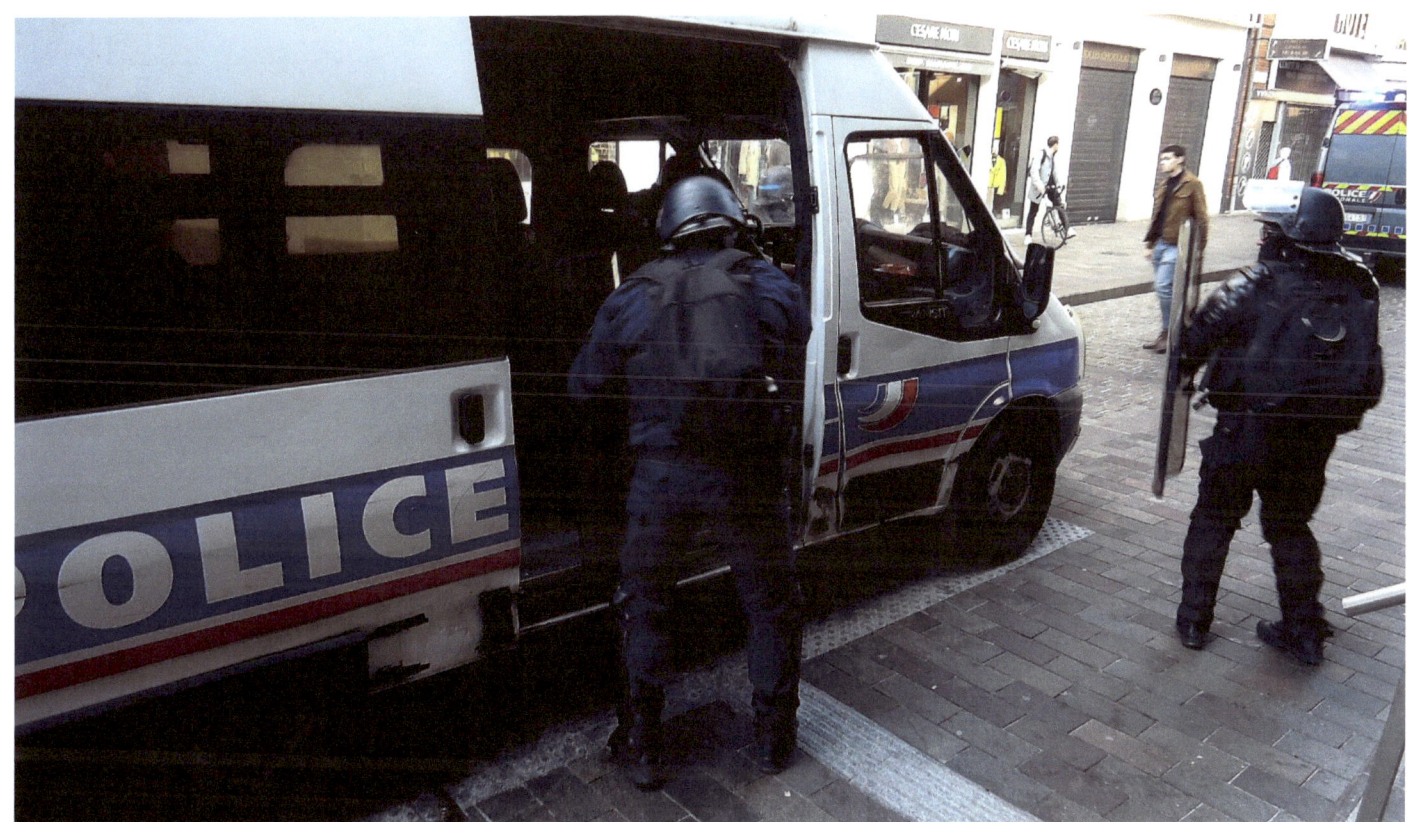

March 28, 2023

Fénétra, a typical dessert made with almond paste, candied lemons and apricot jam. It dates back to the time of the Romans who ate it during the Férétralia, the festival of the dead, together with games and street performances, and is made up of sablé pastry, apricot jam, candied lemon cubes and almonds. For the inhabitants of the city it has become the Sunday dessert.

Since 1963, the artisan pastry chefs of the Toulouse region have celebrated the cake at the end of June with the Fête du Fénétra. It is also a travel cake, as it is easily transportable and can be stored for several days at room temperature.

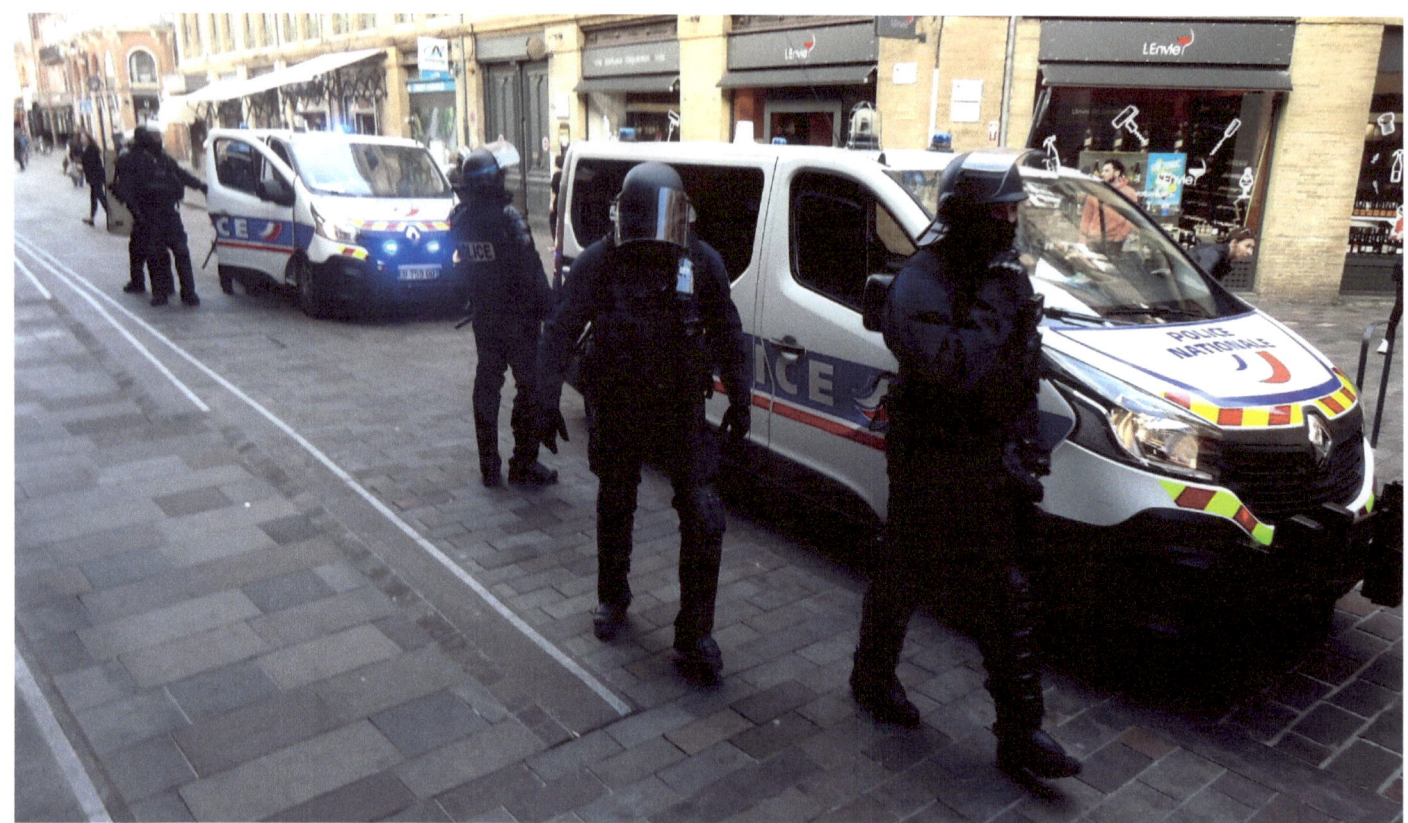

March 28, 2023

The Campidoglio pavé is a delicious dark chocolate morsel with orange praline.

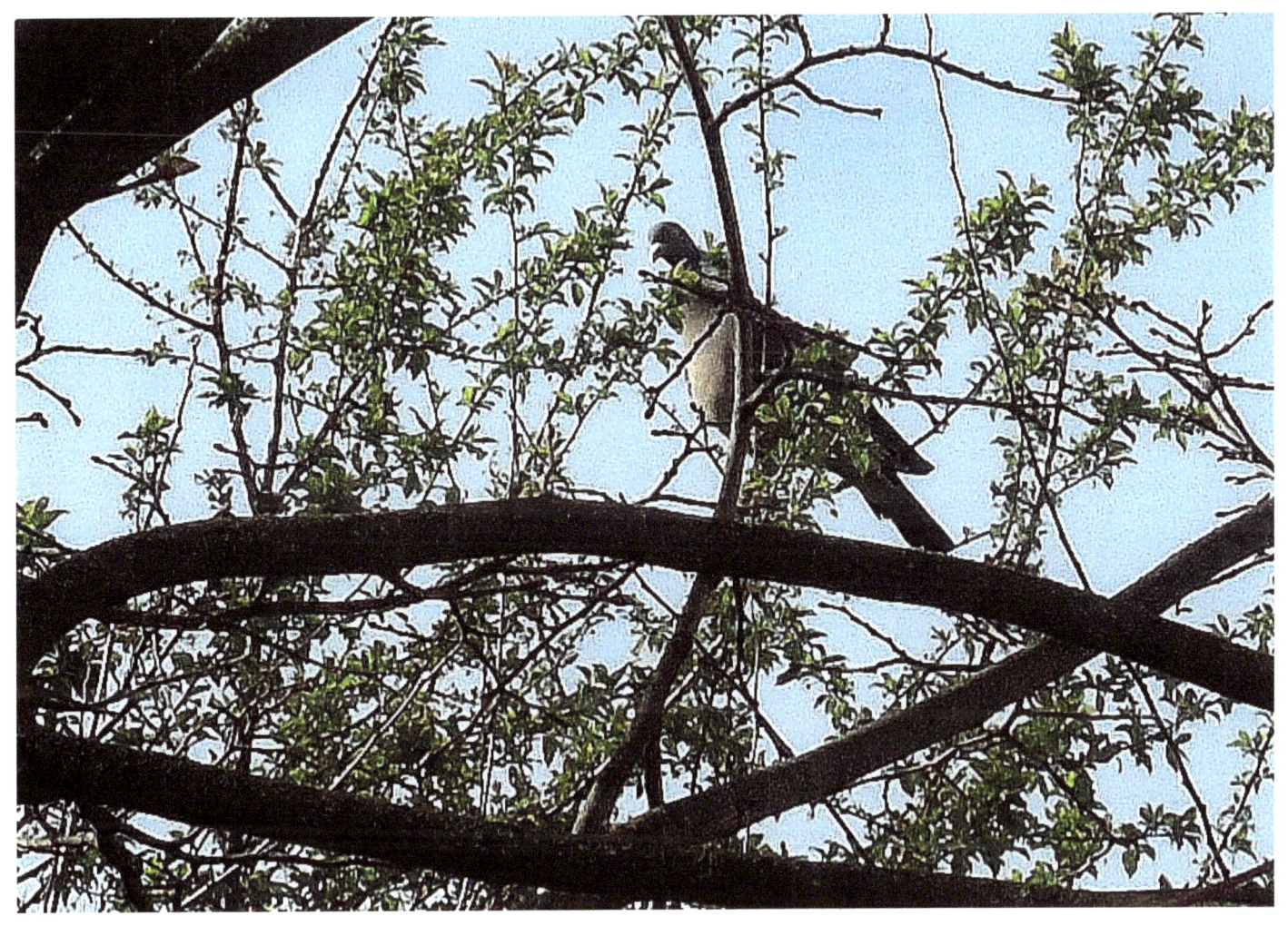

The Capitol brick is a small brick-shaped bon bon with puff pastry and praline.

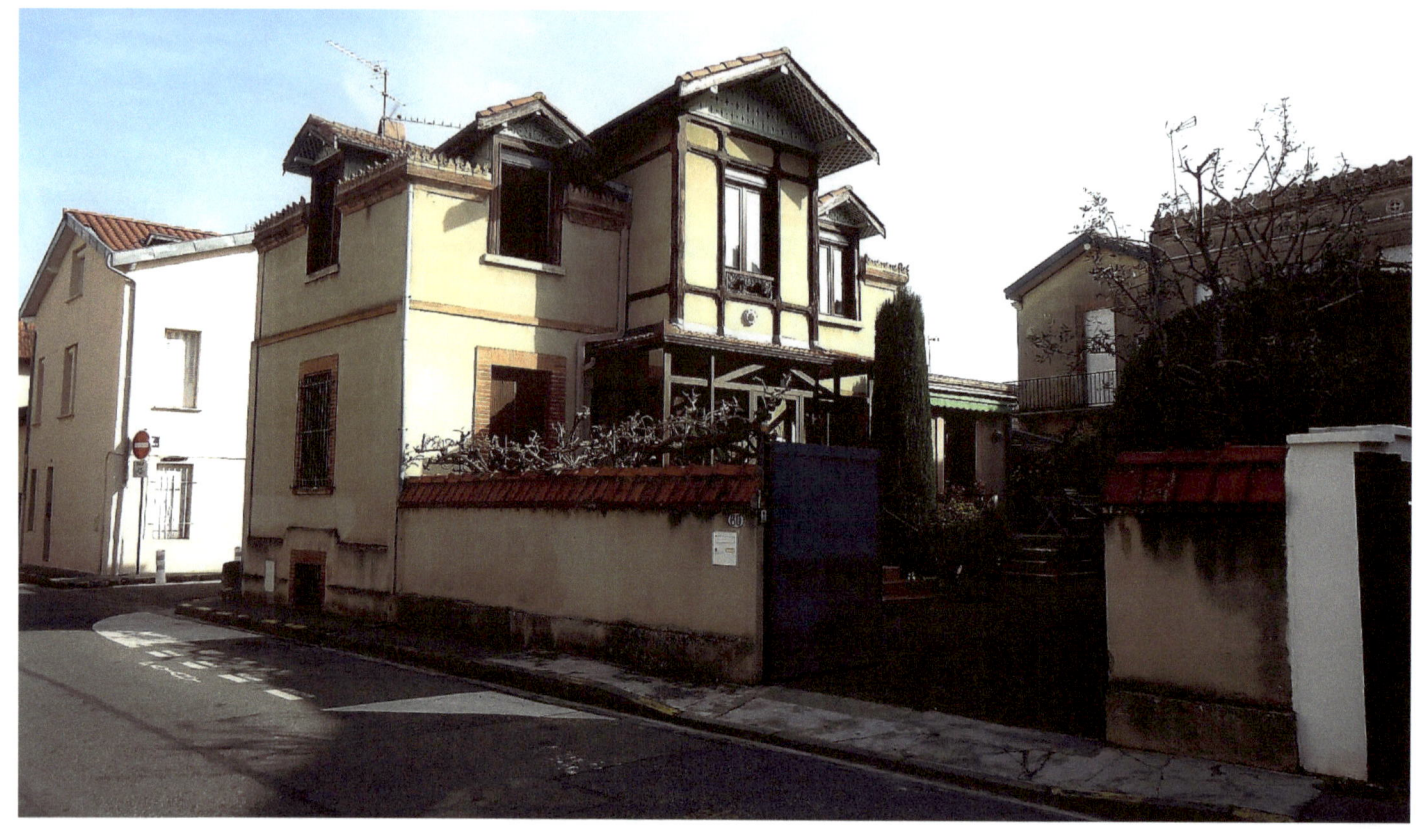

Cheeses occupy an important position in the gastronomy of Toulouse: starting with the famous and tasty Roquefort, made of blue cheese and produced with sheep's milk, or the soft Rocamadour made of goat's milk.

Less known, but very good are Gensac (raw milk goat's cheese with a natural rind from Midi-Pyrenees, near Toulouse), Perail (raw milk sheep's cheese with a natural rind), Pavé Toulousain (raw milk , raw and pressed cow's cheese), and Bleu d'Hougarou (blue cheese made from raw sheep's milk from the Hautes Pyrenees, south of Toulouse).

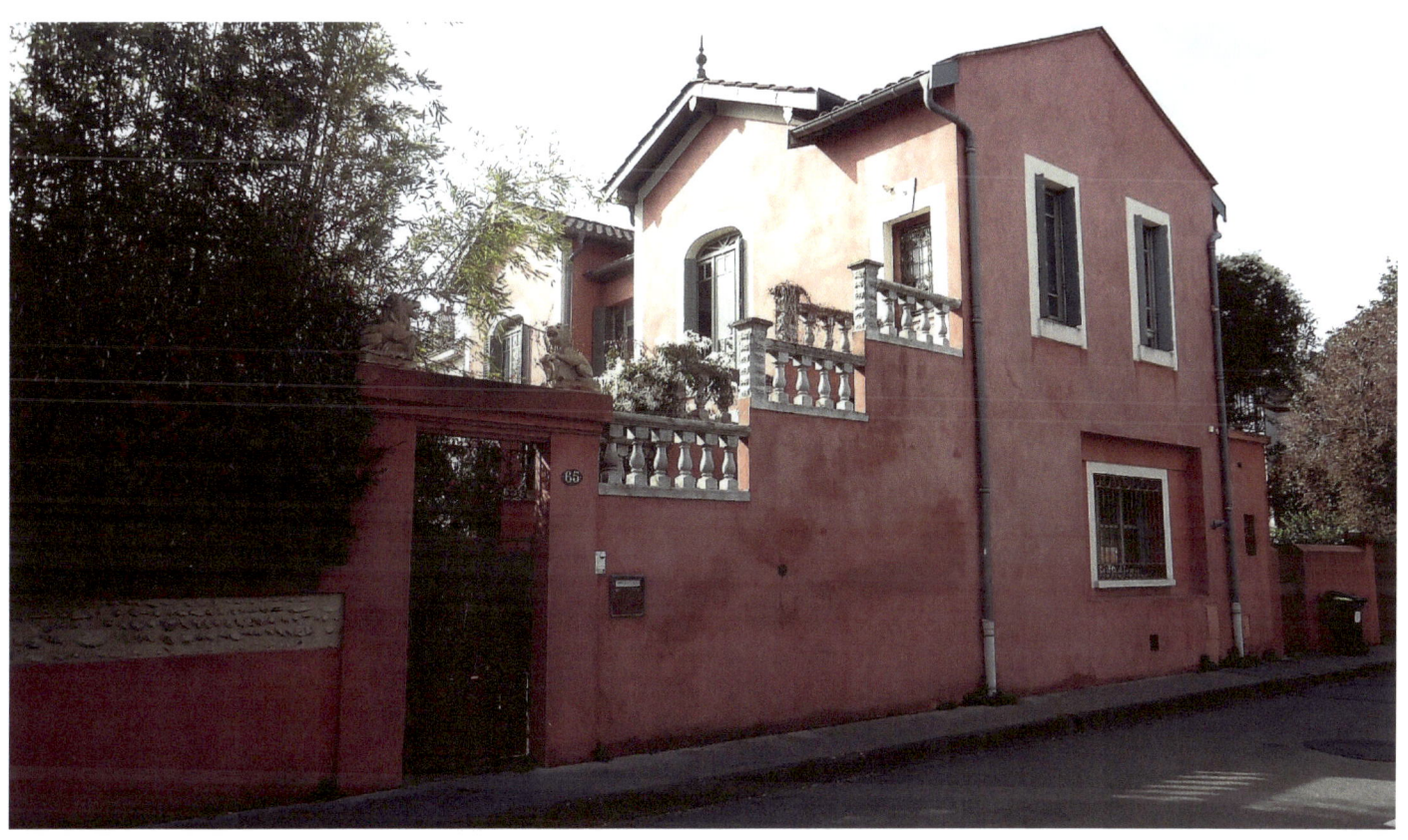

Gaillac wines. For over 2000 years you can ask in Toulouse to drink local wine, which will certainly be a Gaillac - white or red or rosé or sparkling. This is a production from the area north-east of the city, active since the Gallo-Roman era and continued over the centuries also thanks to the Benedictine monks.

As AOC (Appéllation d'Origine Controlée) it dates back to 1938 for white and 1970 for red.

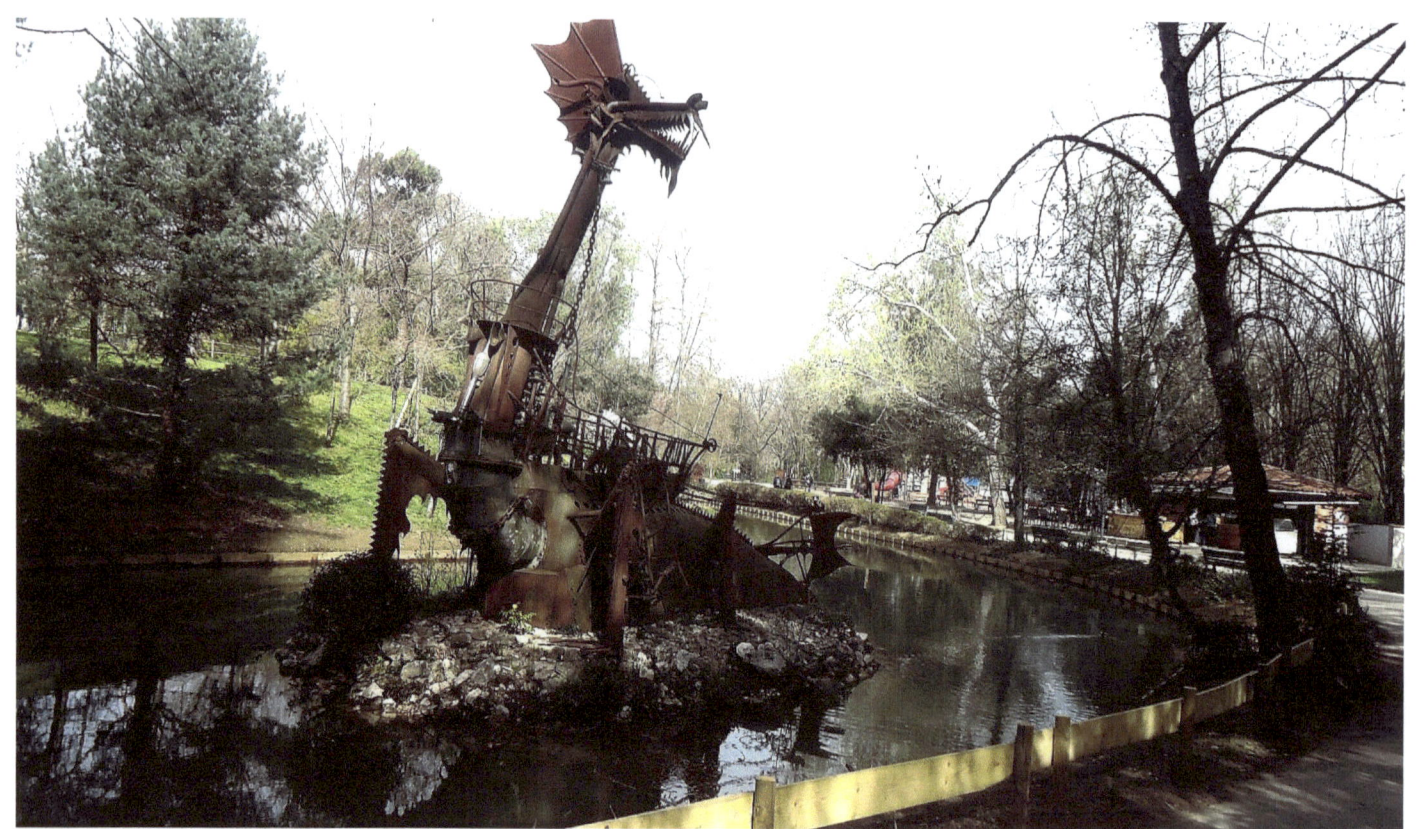

Jardin Japonais Pierre Baudis

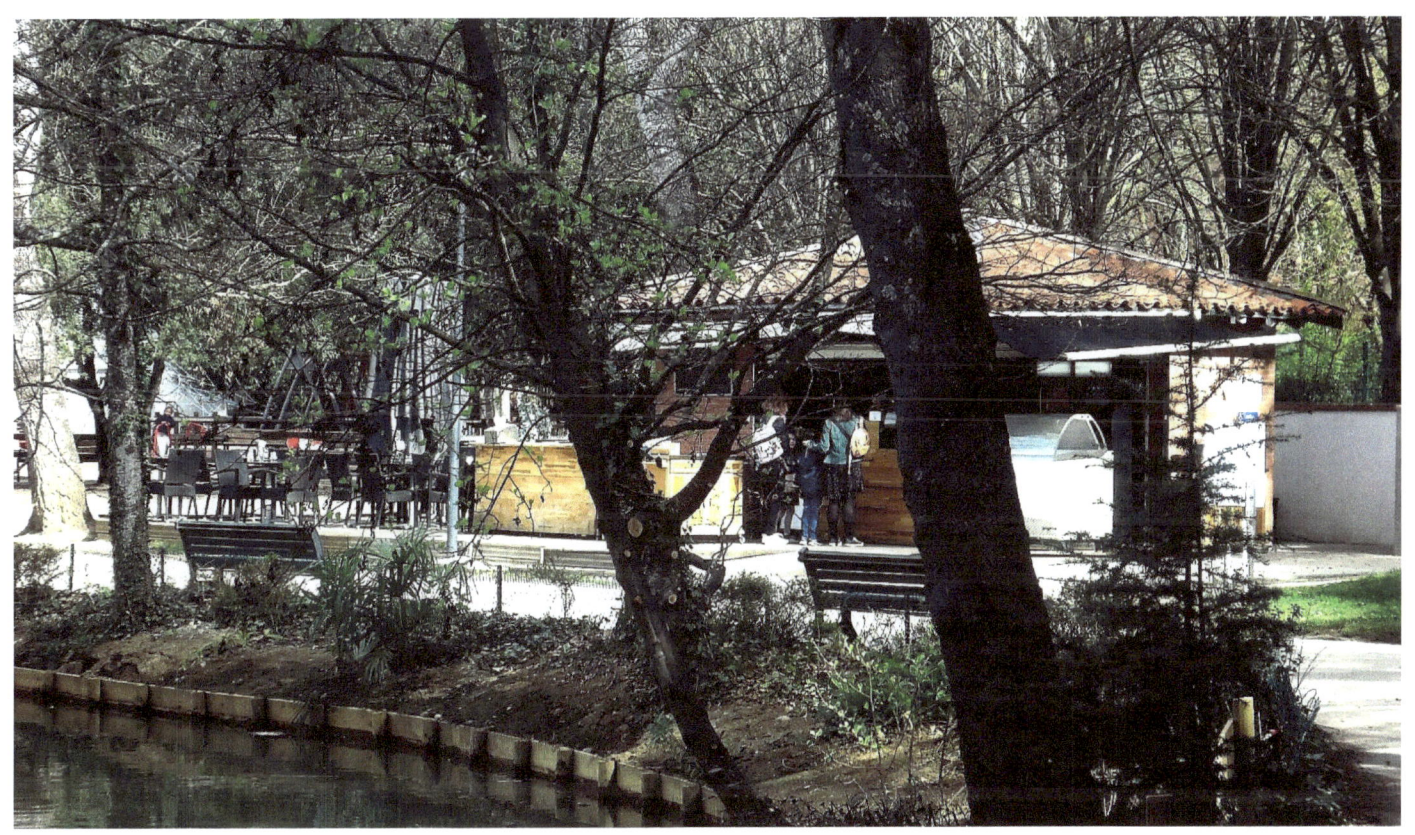

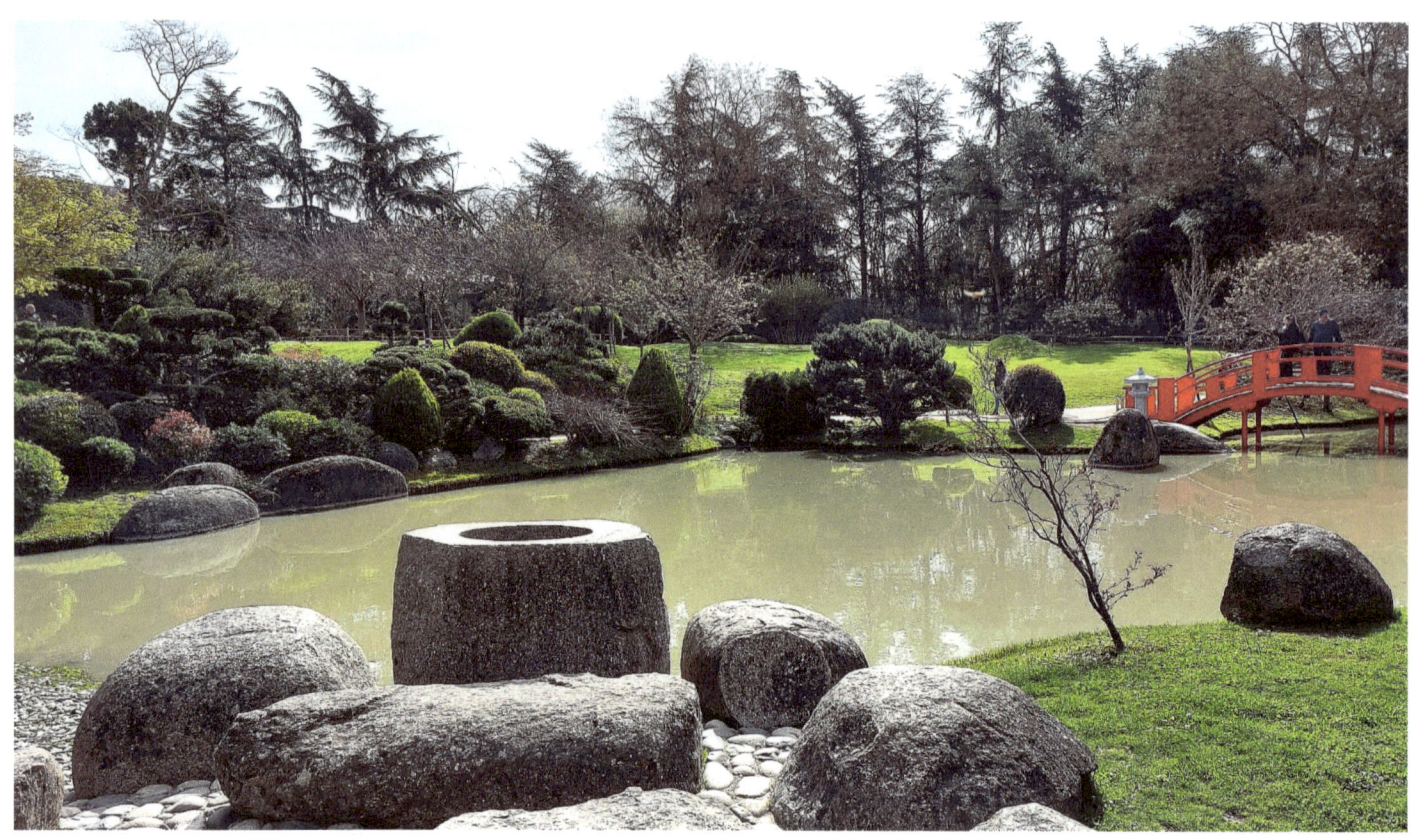

Jardin Japonais Pierre Baudis

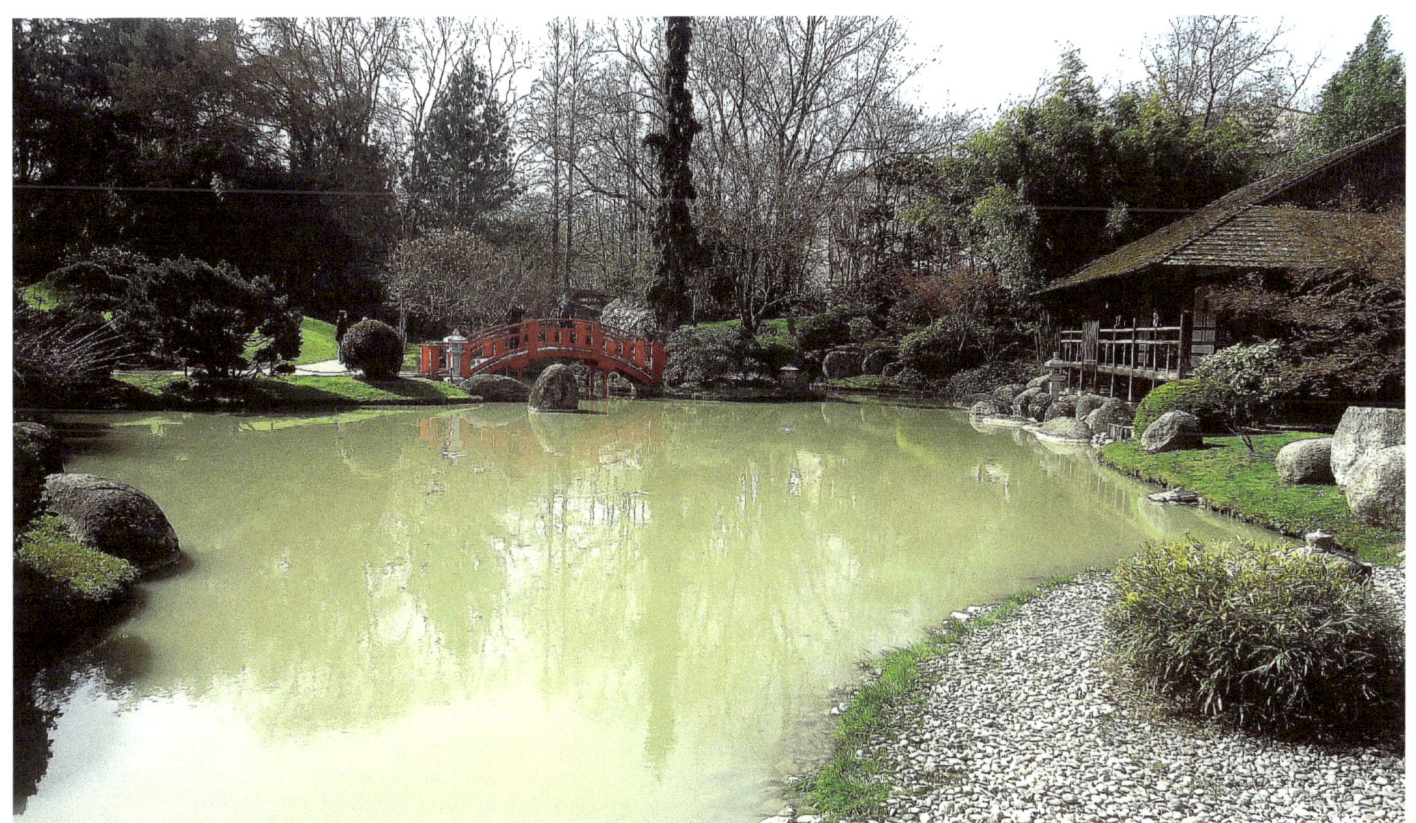

Jardin Japonais Pierre Baudis

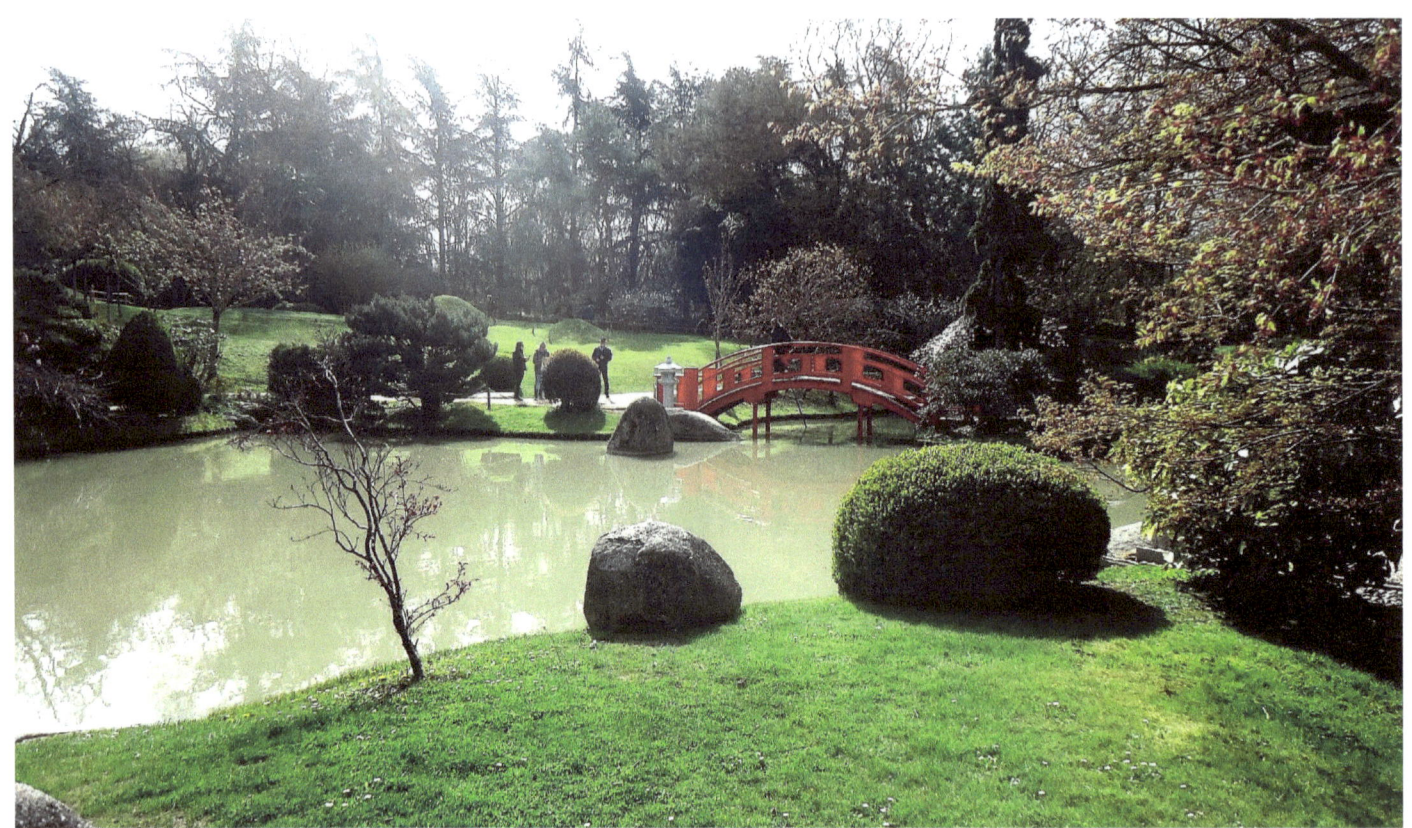

Jardin Japonais Pierre Baudis

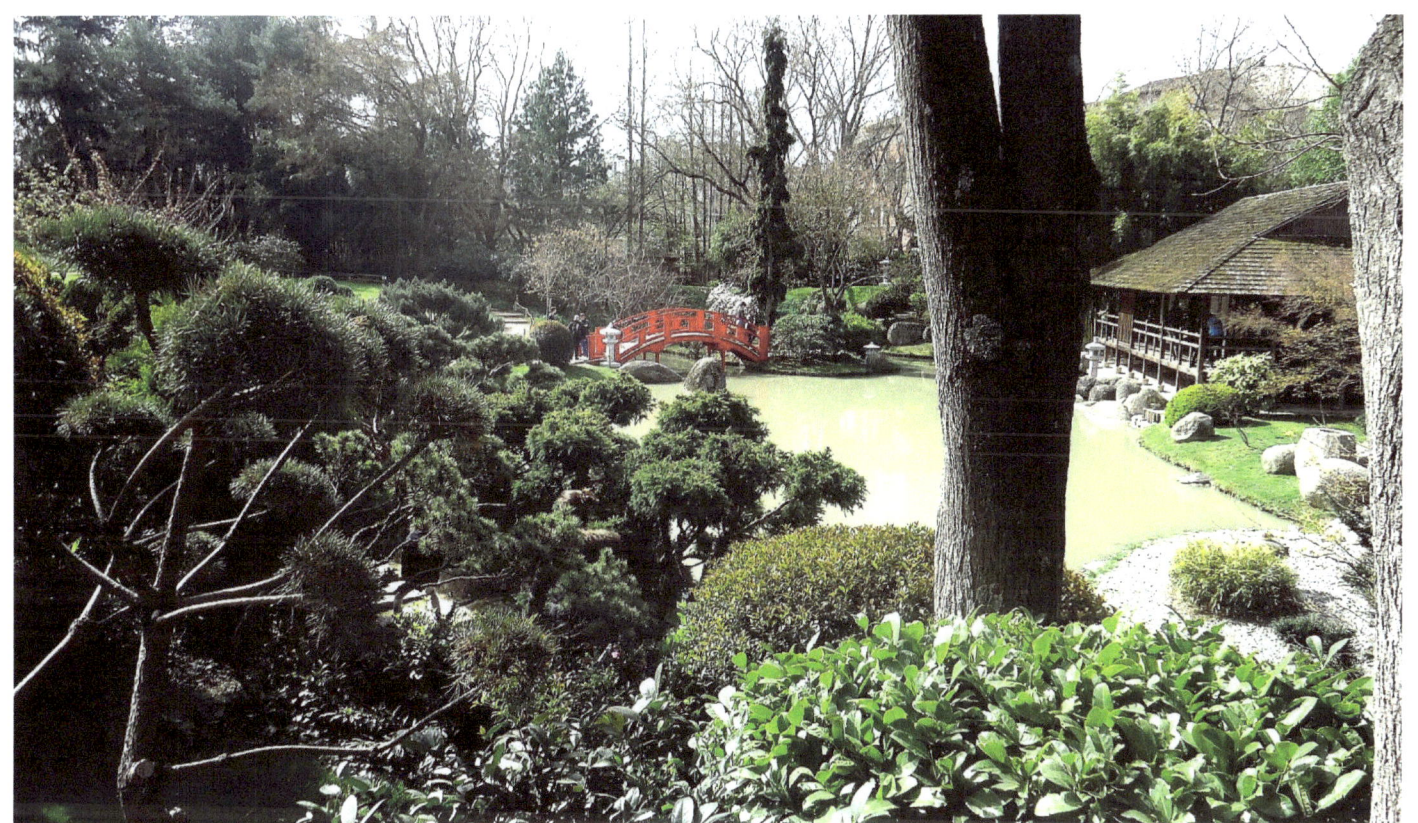

Jardin Japonais Pierre Baudis

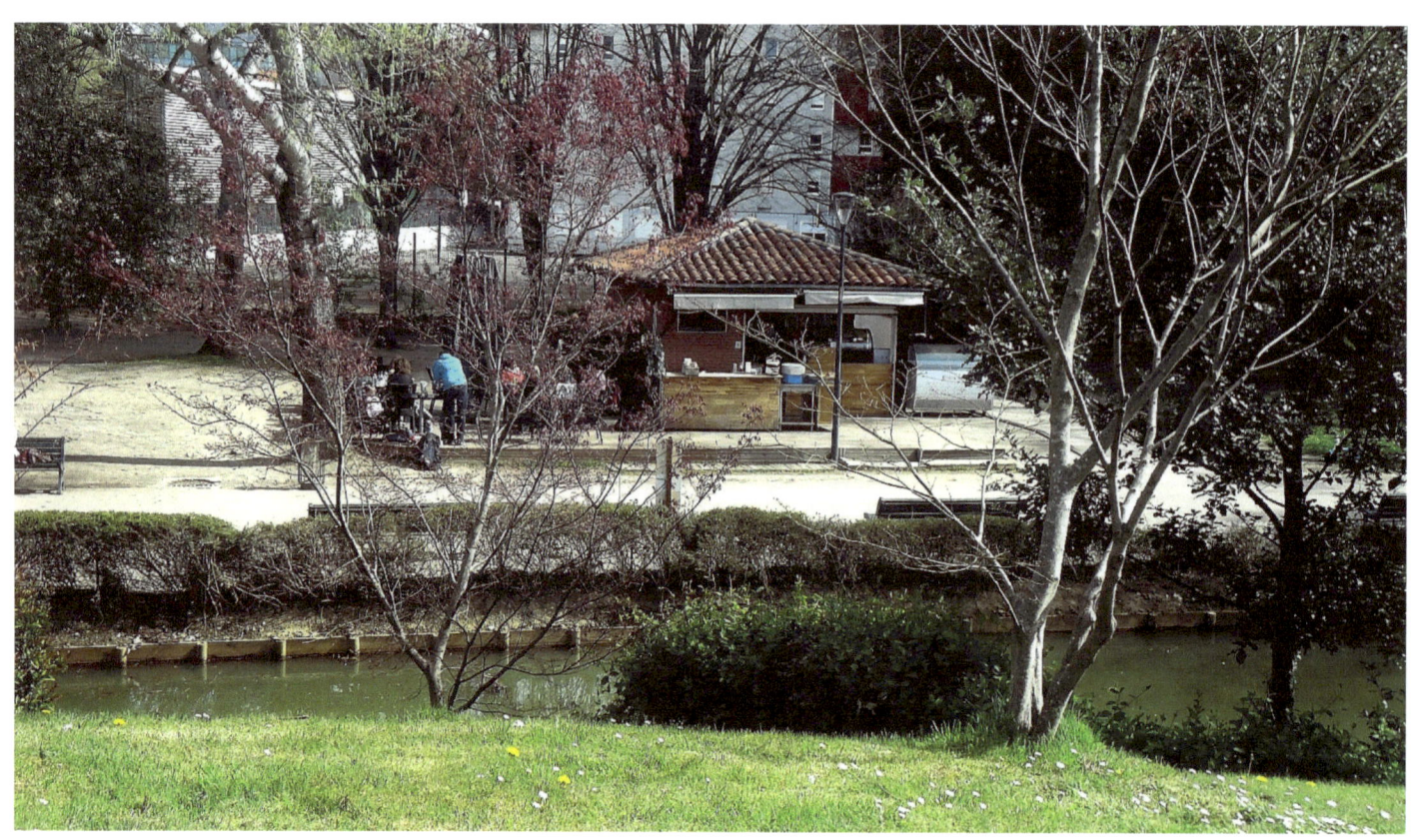

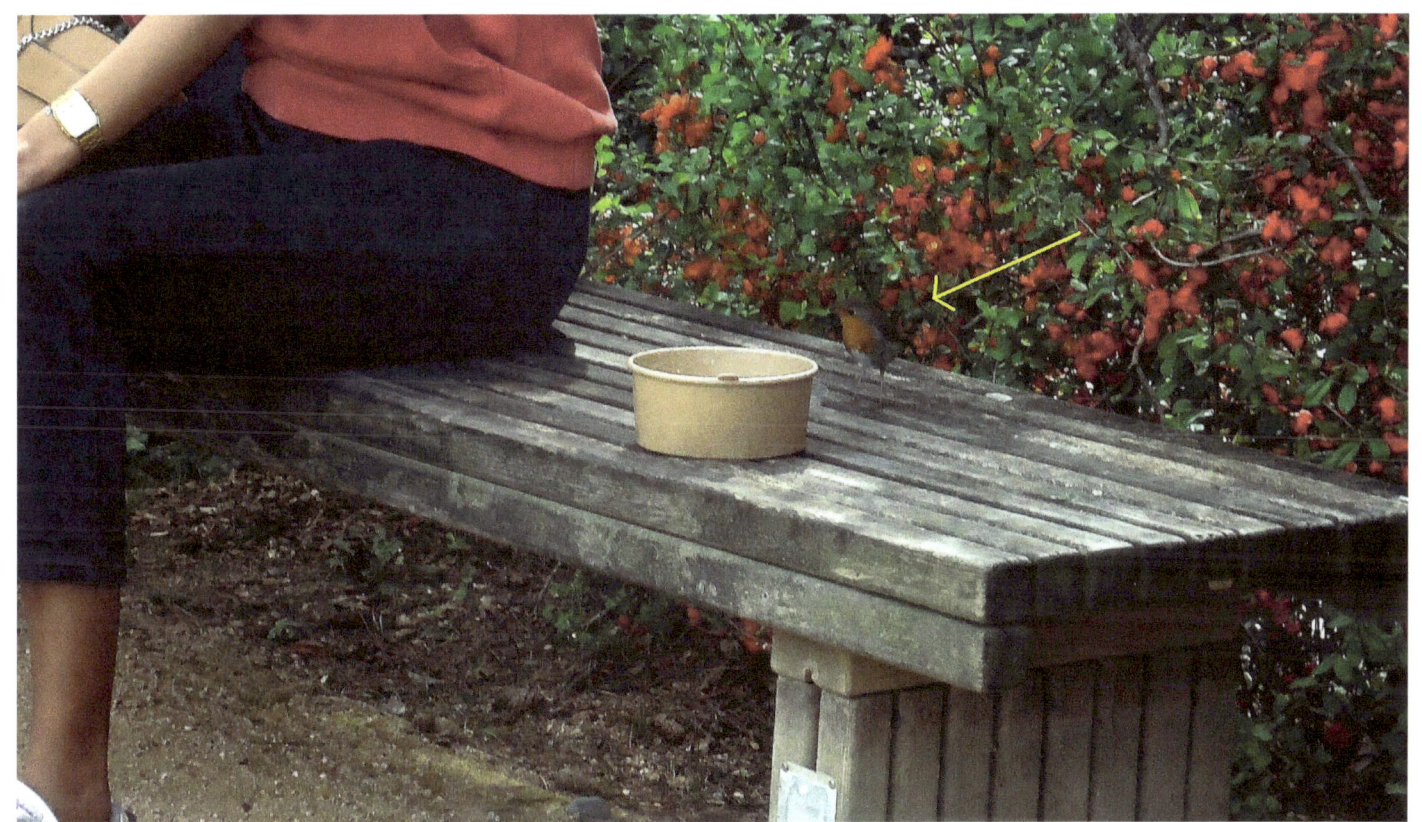

Jardin Japonais Pierre Baudis

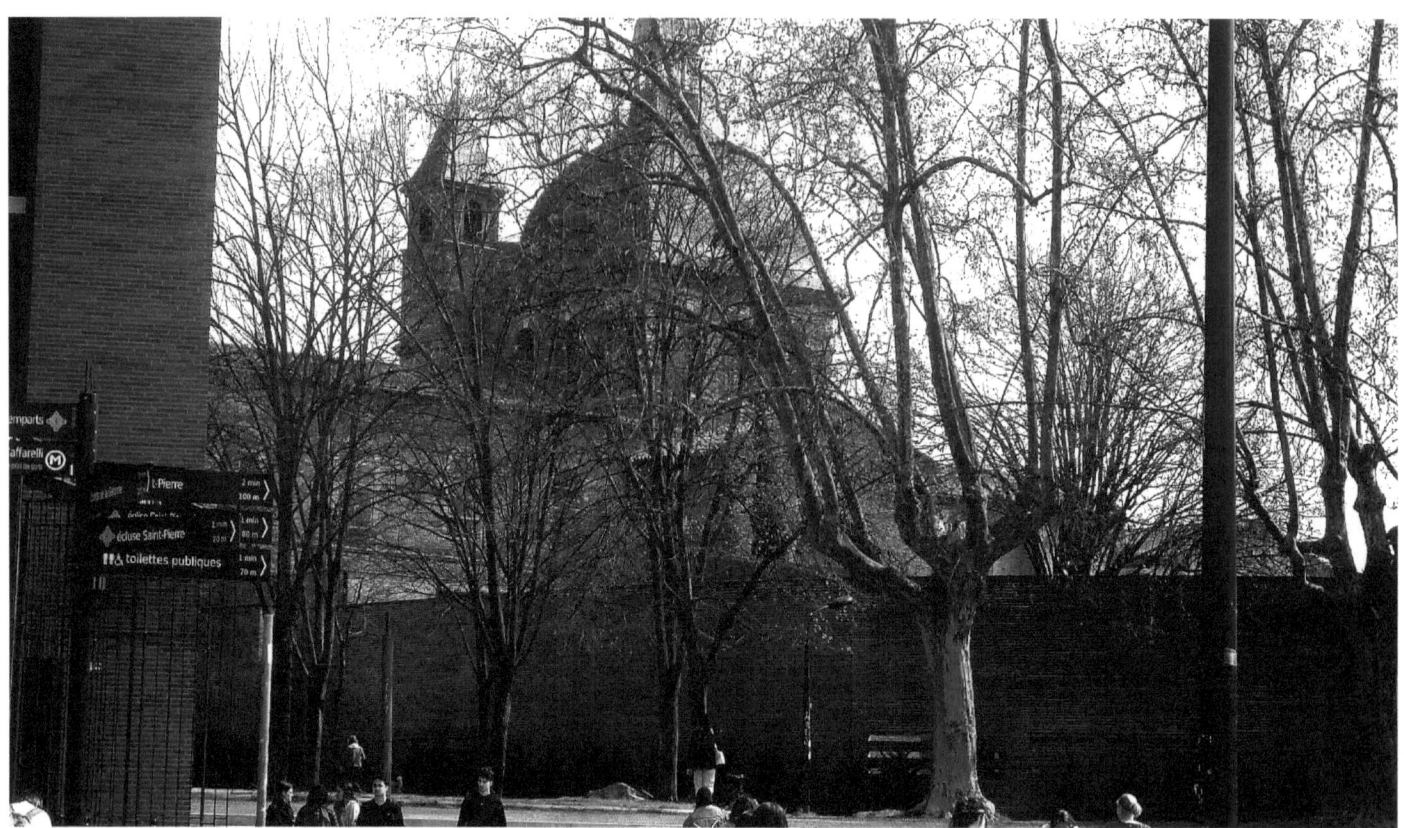

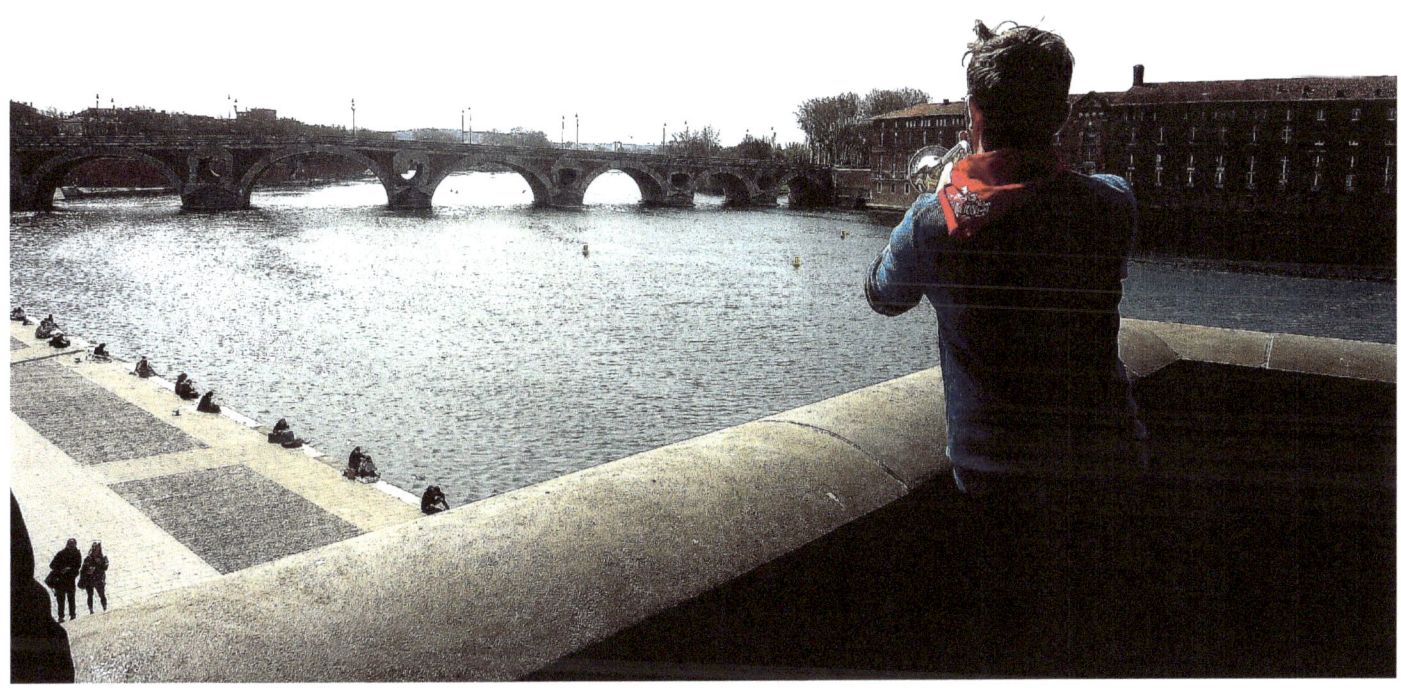

The Pont Neuf over the Garonne

The **Garonne** is a large river in southwestern France that flows in France for 528 km.

It originates from the Pyrenees in Spanish territory, flows north-east, after which it crosses Toulouse, from where it is flanked up to the mouth by the Canal du Midi. Finally it reaches Bordeaux arriving near its mouth, which is in the Atlantic Ocean, joined to that of the Dordogne, giving rise to the large Gironde estuary.

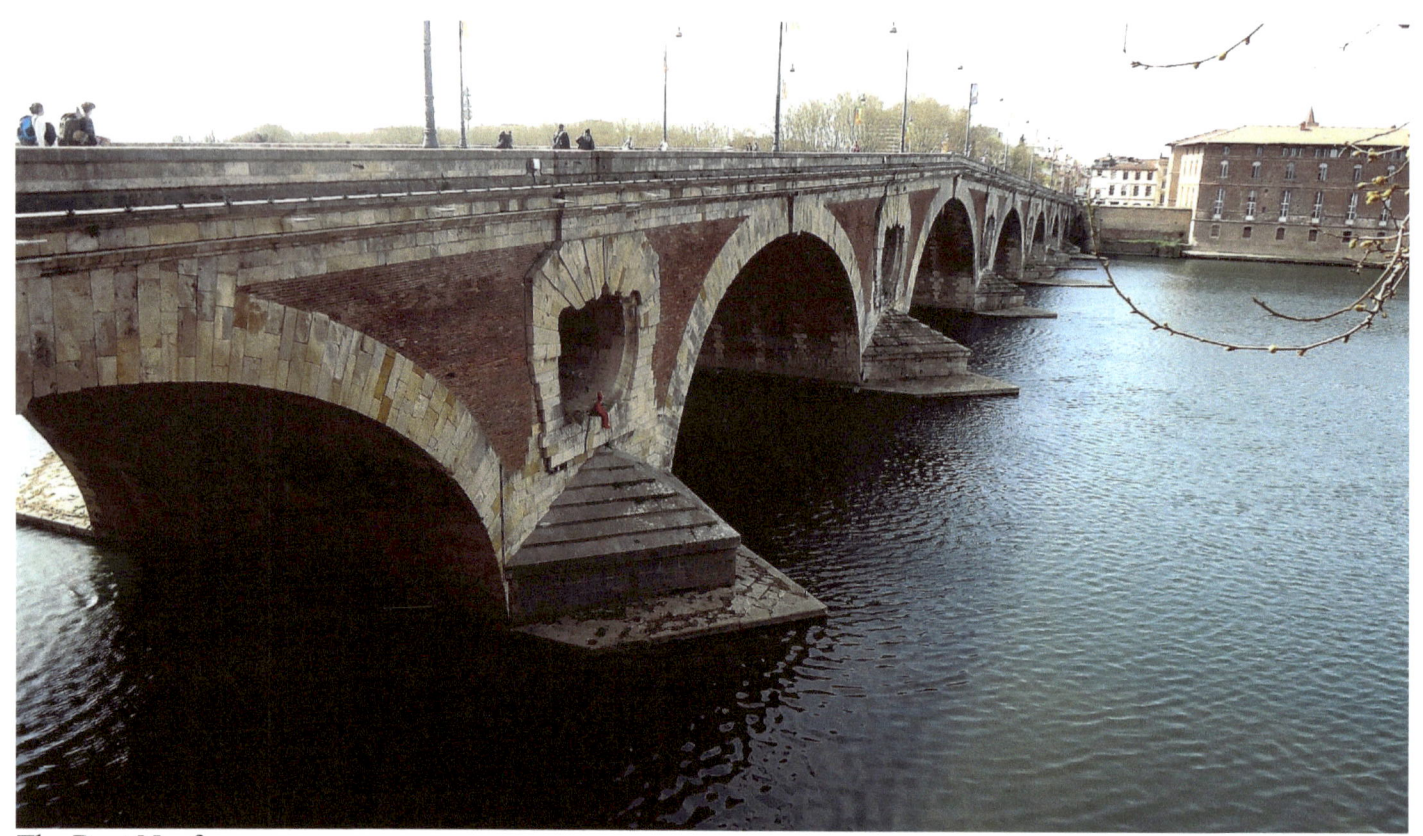

The Pont Neuf

Construction work on the **Pont Neuf** began in 1544, but was interrupted in 1560 by the Wars of Religion, resumed only in 1632 and inaugurated in 1659 by King Louis XIV.

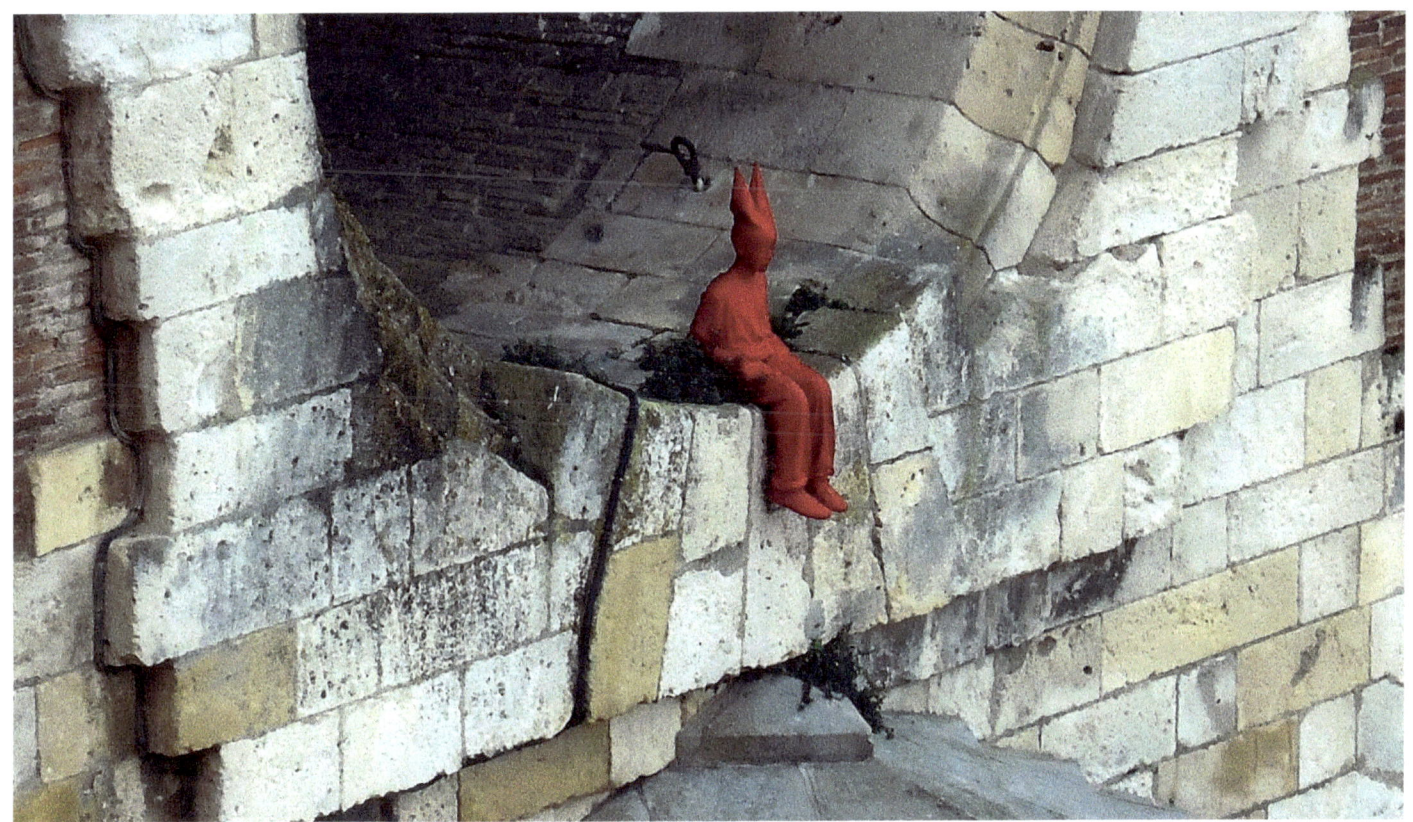

The Pont Neuf

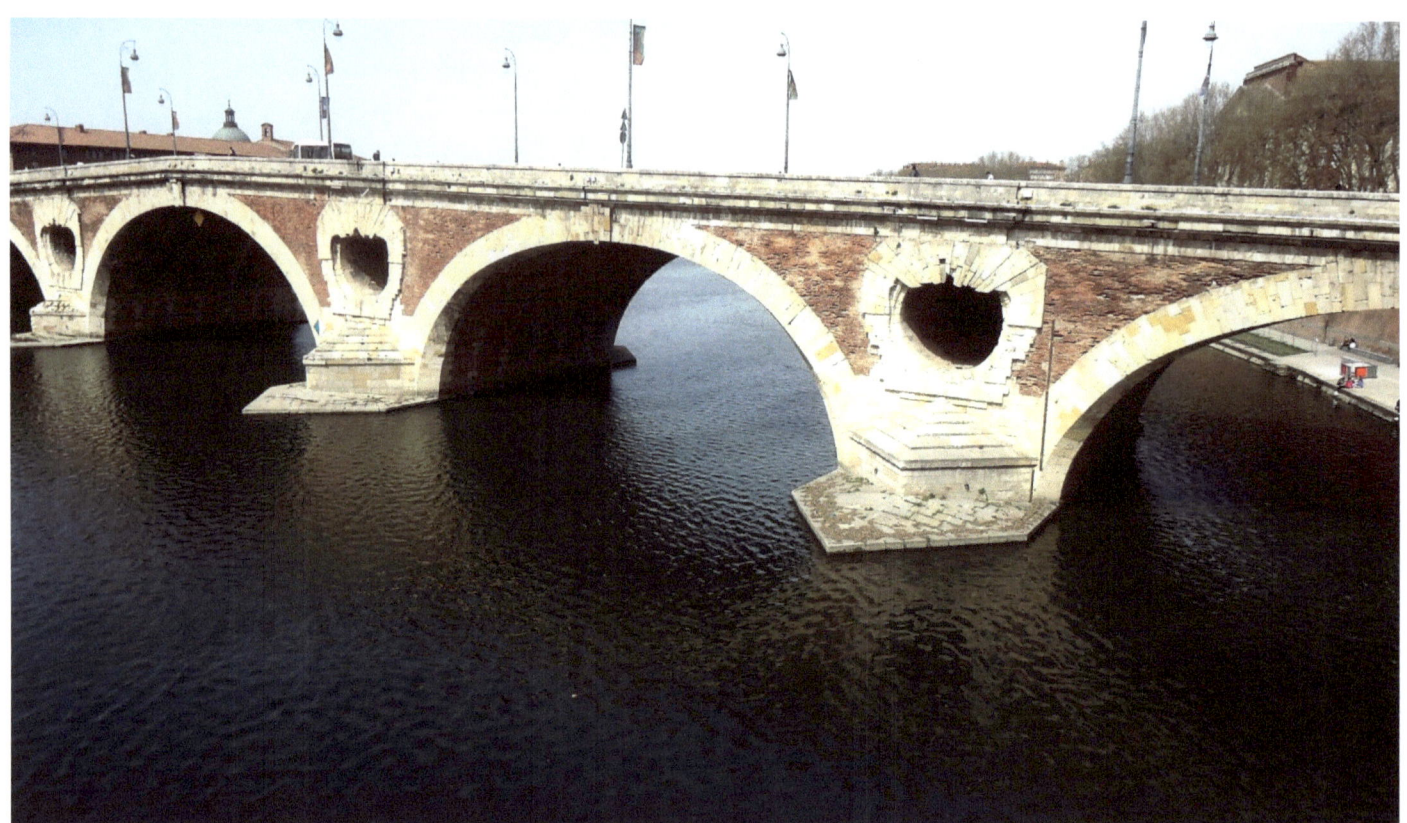

The Pont Neuf

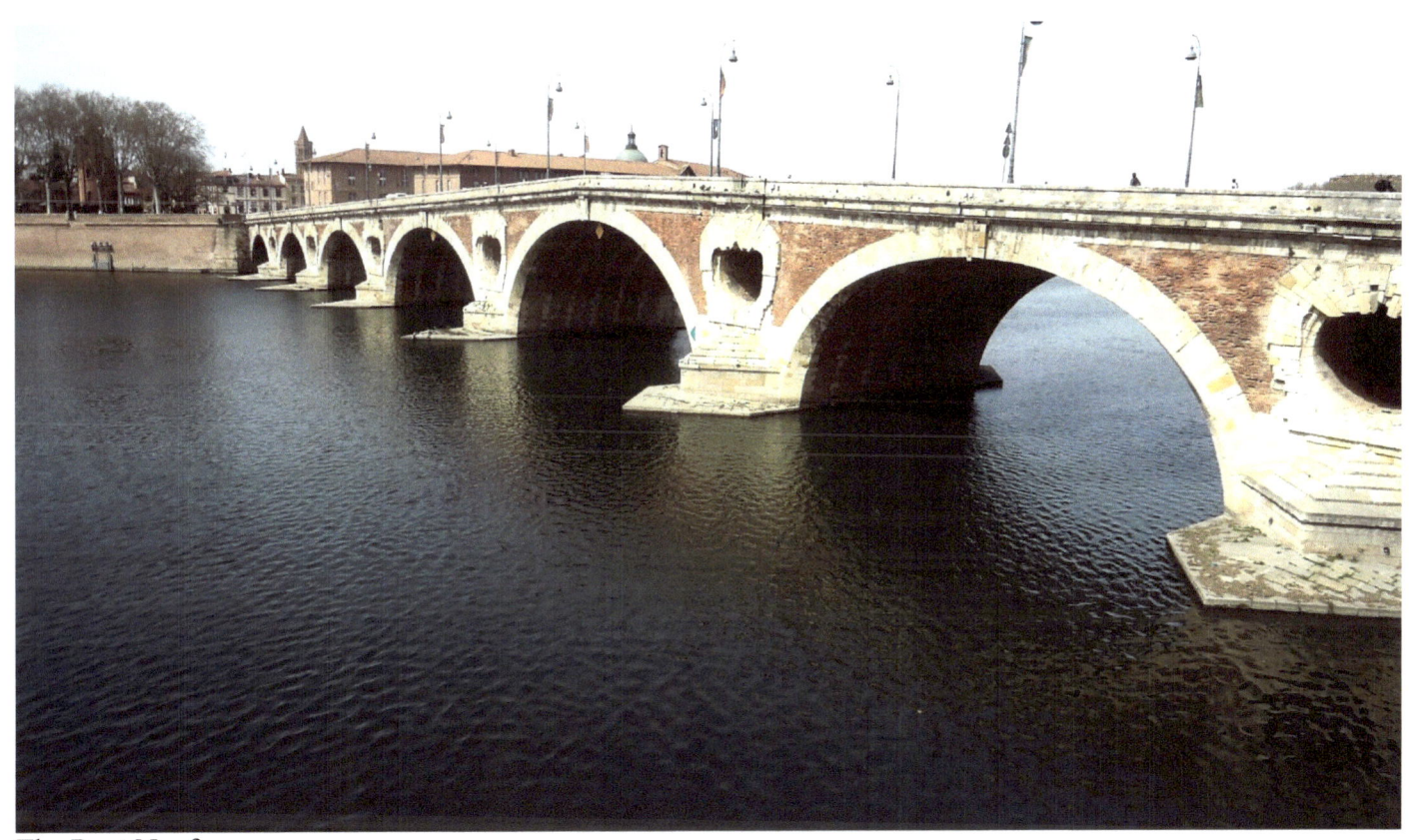

The Pont Neuf

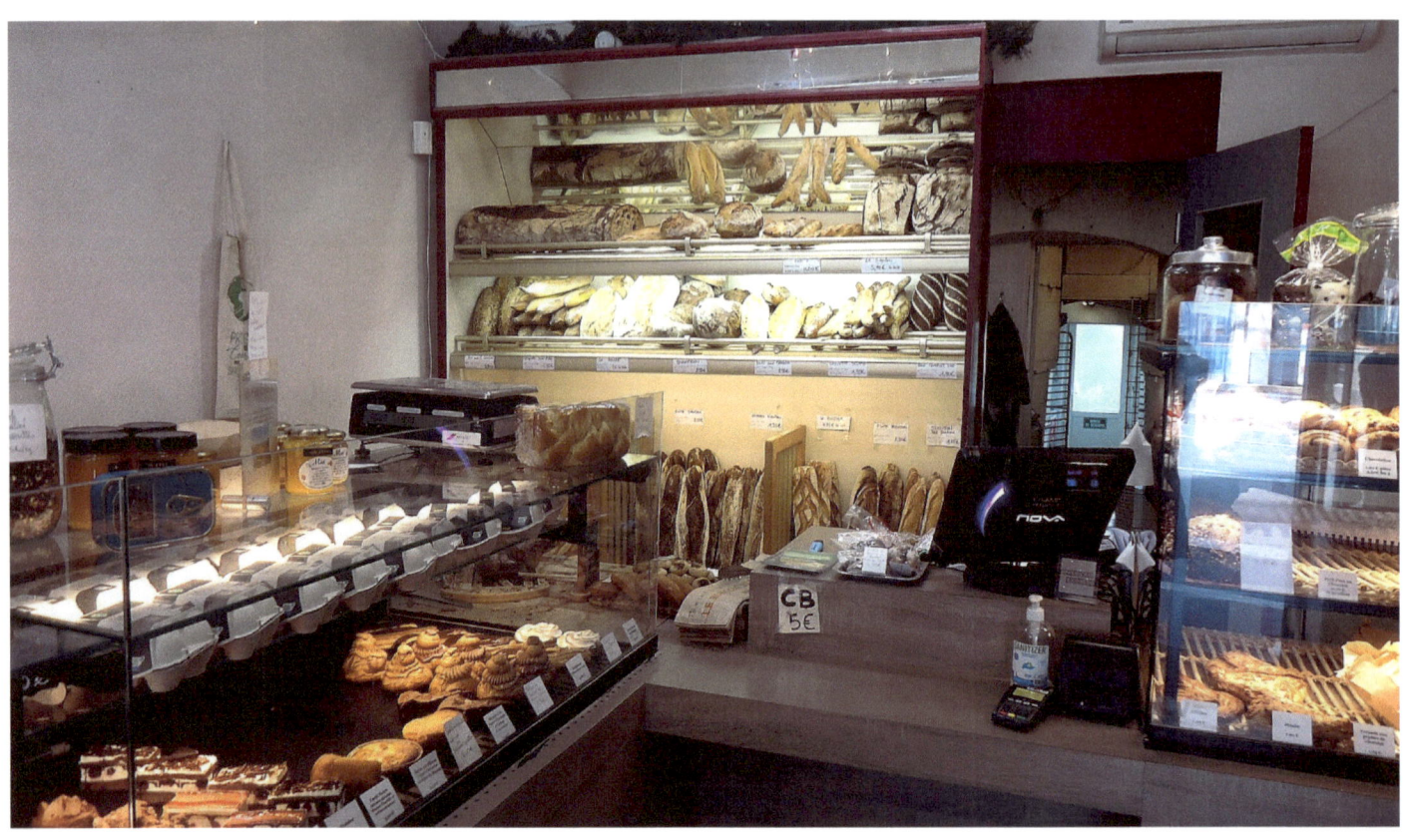

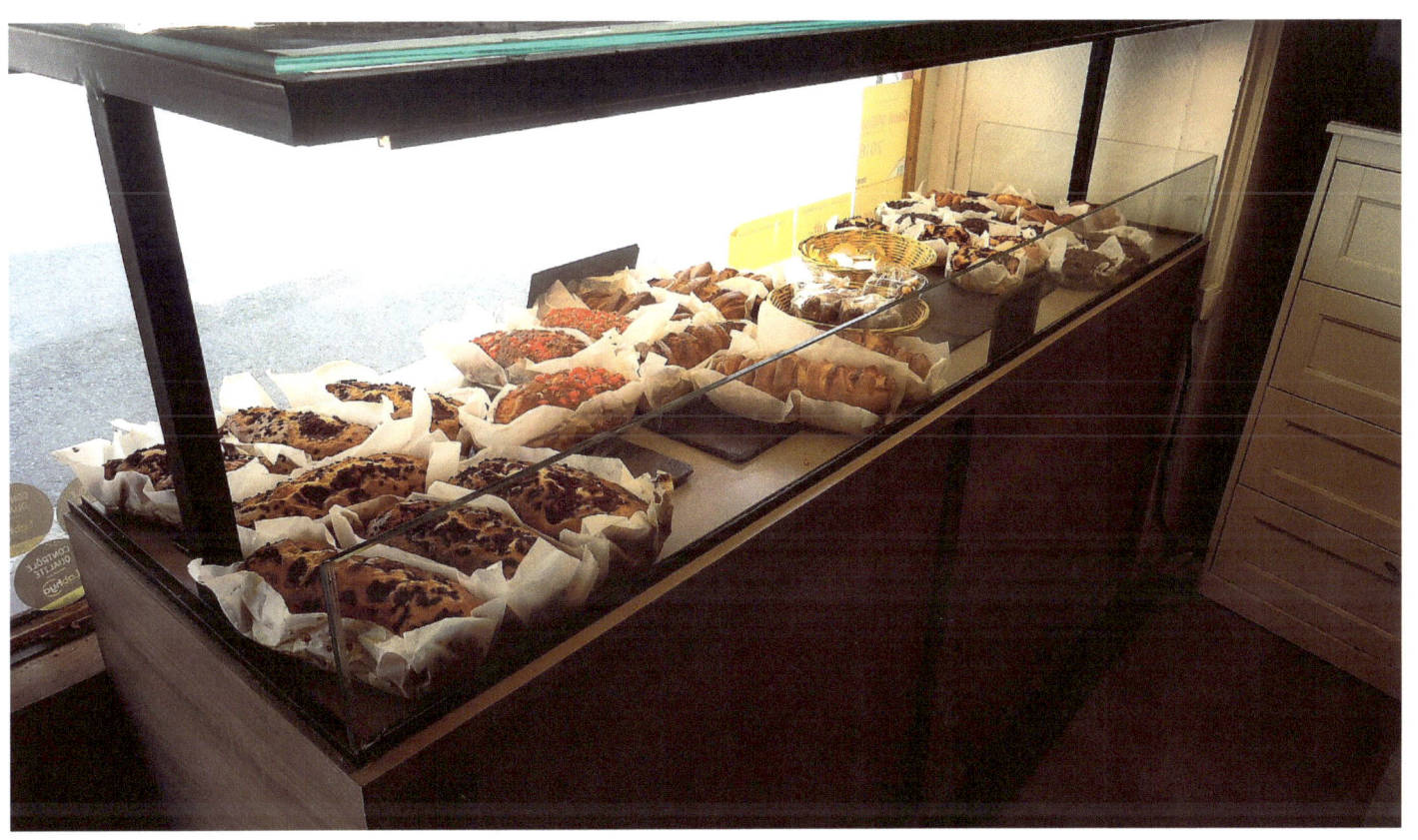

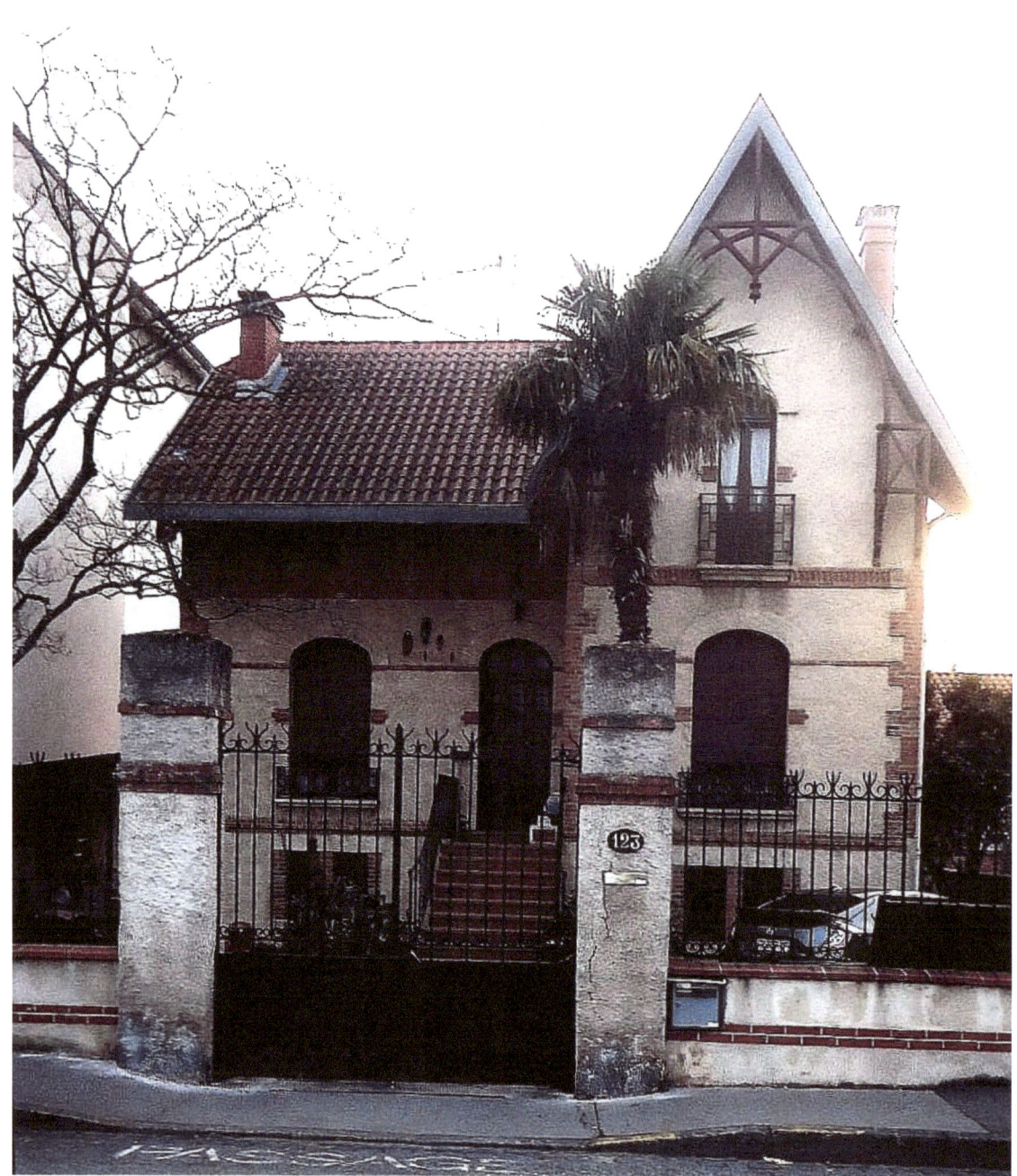